Walk of a Lifetime

Front and back cover photographs by Curtis Cowles
Cover design by Theresa Thomas

Printed in the United States of America

Second Edition, 2024

ISBN 978-0-915725-05-2

WALK OF A LIFETIME

AN INSPIRATIONAL JOURNEY

From a shattered dream to the Cincinnati Bearcats

By Alex Meacham with Sam Dunn & Mark Brown

TABLE OF CONTENTS

ACKNOWLEDGMENTS

First and foremost I would like to thank my mother and father. They have always been in my corner, through all my ups and downs, never losing faith in me. I would like to thank my brother, Tony, for being a positive role model in my life. To my Grandmother, who always tells me to enjoy life each and every day. And to the rest of my family; Aunt Muriel, Uncle Brother, Aunt Mary, Tony, Tiffany and Zoe VanJohnson, and Amy Meacham.

Thanks to Coach Huggins for giving me the opportunity to be a part of the best basketball program in America. No matter what anyone says, he is the best college coach around! To Simon Anderson, thank you for taking on this project and having faith in it and me. I have learned so much from this experience; Mark Brown, thank you for agreeing to be involved with this book. We couldn't have done it with out you; Sam Dunn, thank you for being my biggest supporter, since day one! This is just the start of many things to come for us. And Jerome Gray for being my mentor on and off the court. Thanks for all the "hand-me down knowledge."

I would also like to thank Willie C. Jackson, Doherty Middle School, Tom Betts, Ed Wiseman, Seven Hills High School, Dick "Duke" Snyder, Coaches Stowers and Derckson, Purcell Marian High School, Coach Gergen, Roger Bacon High School, Father Roger, Father Dennis, Mrs. Coyle, Brother Gene, Coach Brewer, Coach Starkey, Jim "Bubs" Kindt, Mr. Grosser, Mr. McGrath, Brother Conrad, the rest of the Bacon faculty and staff.

Also thanks to Coach Herald and the Walnut Hills Basketball program, Mitch Perdrix, Dave Walker, Sean Hanarahan, Brian Laake, Damon Martin, Seth Coyle and the Coyle Family, Lori Gray, Kenny Cole, The ATO's, Tabari McCoy, Matt Burgen, Dr. Sherman, Matt Drane (It's your turn now), Dave Patania, Ed Marks, Mike Sanders, Jane Anne and Larry Carter, Mr. Hull and the Hull family.

Thanks to the University of Cincinnati, the students and fans, the Shoemaker Center Staff, Tim Swanger, Sean Cooley, Scott Greenawalt, Mickey Marotti, Craig Porte, Beth Anne, Bruce Ivory, Stephanie Rousseau, Shelly Dixon, Chris Byron, Carol Wissman, Ray Harrison, Jim Burbridge, Gail Stocker, Dr. Porte, Lt. Crawford, Hal, Diane, Jeremy and Aaron Fishbein, Jayde Grossman, Dr. Colosimo, Dr. Ellis, Dr. Stephens, Corey Brinn, Mark Berger, Joe Lucas, Scott Wilhoit, Chuck Machuck, George Van Benko, Terry Nelson, John Sheffield, Paul Klaczak, Brian Mand, Janie Shaffer, Bill Mulvihill, Pat Eaves, Steve Moeller, Hiawatha Francisco, Meagan Kantor, Cynthia Oaxley, Tom Hathaway, Brian McCann, Bob Goin, Dr. Steger, Coach Baker, Mick Cronin, John Loyer, Dan Peters, Larry Harrison, Chris Goggins, Frank Jessie, Winona Shaw-Gunn and Rene Heroux.

Thanks to all the walk-ons before me, you made this possible. All my teammates, past and present. To Jean Stephens, who died while this book was in progress, thanks for being that smile in the hallway every day after practice. Mike DeCourcy, Paul Daugherty, Dan Hoard, Anthony Buford, Lance McAlister, everyone at 700 WLW, Jerry Fitgerald, Steve Massielo, Josh Partner, Global Lead, Curtis Cowles, Theresa Thomas, Glenn Riley, and the entire city of Cincinnati.

Alex Meacham

First and foremost I would like to thank my mother for believing in my dreams and never pulling me down from out of the clouds. I would also like to thank my dad and my two sisters, Evonna and Kalynn ("Bert"), for all their support. I definitely can't forget about my Aunt K-Kay who at times can be a bit much, but has been there since day one.

A big thank you goes out to my second family—Mike, Carla, and Ben Arnold.

I would really like to say thank you to Mrs. Sue Dokter and her husband, Paul, who over the years have helped me develop my writing skills.

Thank you, Christina, for reading this book when it was in the really "ruff" stages.

A special thank you goes out to Brian ("Yogi") and Melissa who have been great friends. And to my friend, Curt, who 1 respect very much for always telling me the truth.

To my silent inspiration who inspires me in everything I do, I have to say thank you very much for keeping me focused. Hopefully, this is just the beginning to everything we have talked about. M. L. P.

1 only have one page to write thank you's, so to all of those who were not mentioned, please know that you have a special place in my heart, and I appreciate everything you have done for me.

Sam Dunn

A thanks to Global Lead Management Consulting for their unyielding support of office space, time, and—yes, paper,

A special thanks to the Cincinnati Herald newspaper for providing me with the opportunity to cover sports in a unique, informative, and enjoyable manner. Without you, my role in this project would never have been possible.

To everyone (too many to mention, but you know who you are) who has supported my writing endeavors throughout the years, 1 will always be grateful. While I would love to name everyone individually, I am so afraid I might miss that one special person.

With that in mind, let me simply say thank you, and may God bless each and everyone of you.

Mark Brown

FOREWORD

Alex Meacham is why the term student-athlete came into our vocabulary. A student who loved athletics, more specifically in Alex's case, basketball. An athlete who poured all his energy and exuberance into his passion. We have many students who would love the limelight, love the adulation, love the exposure, and loaf the work.

My greatest appreciation for Alex comes because of the two loves we both share. One is, naturally, a love of this great game; and two, a love for this University and city. Alex represented his University and his city with the dedication and fervor they both deserve.

Alex volunteered his time, effort, and dedication at a time when we needed it most. When we were short on scholarship bodies, and ridiculed and deserted by many fans and media alike because of an internal investigation, Alex's love for the University and the basketball program never waved, in fact, it grew stronger.

This is a story of a hometown kid who went to college in our city and represented all that is good about intercollegiate athletics.

Alex will forever have a place in my heart for his love and dedication to our University, city, basketball program, and to our coaching staff. This is his story so enjoy it as much as I have.

Bob Huggins
Head Basketball Coach

DEFINITION

Before reading this book, I think it is important that you know what a walk-on athlete is. Almost every collegiate sport has a walk-on. Baseball, football, soccer, tennis, etc.

... in my case the sport is basketball

There are usually 12-15 players on a college basketball team. To be one of those players at the University of Cincinnati is special.

I was not recruited nor did I receive a scholarship. Usually scholarship athletes get a free education, room, and board. I received none of that. I worked for free. Why? I love the game of basketball.

Off the court there is a difference between a scholarship player and a walk-on. You are the low man on the totem pole, and you have to fight for respect. On the court there isn't any difference. When you lace up your shoes and the ball is rolled out on the court, scholarship or walk-on, you are there to do one job.

There aren't walk-ons in just athletics. They can be found in every area of life. Big companies have interns, colleges have teaching assistants, movies have extras. They may have different names, but they're walk-ons.

I have very few loves in my life. I love my family and close friends. I eventually want to be that "scholarship" player in life, but I loved being a walk-on.

CHAPTER 1

WALKING ON WATER

I was shaking. My palms were sweaty. If someone had asked me if I were all right, I would have said no. I didn't feel sick, even though I had been suffering from the flu for the last two days. I couldn't sit down and I didn't want to stand up for fear that I might have lost my balance. There were only three seconds on the clock, and there was one last chance for a big play. This wasn't just a basketball game for me. This wasn't Cincinnati versus Duke. This was my life.

I was up against tremendous odds with no time to waste, and I made it happen. I made the big play. I chose to lace up my basketball shoes again after not playing for five years. I chose not to listen to everybody who said "can't," and decided that I "could." I chose to walk on to the University of Cincinnati basketball team. I did all of that in a span of three seconds. Three seconds is a lifetime in college basketball, and in those three seconds I saw my life much clearer then I ever did before.

The ref signaled that it was time, so we broke from our huddle. I didn't think that I was going to be able to watch, but I had to. I had the best seat in the house. I was right there. I was on the bench. A place that I gladly accepted because I knew my role. That was a tough role to accept, something that a lot of people can't do so they miss out on a lot of things in life. The whistle blew, and my life from that point was put into play.

While standing there in that moment of glory, I realized I used to think about the guys on the sidelines who never played in the game or set foot on the court, but cheered and celebrated just as much as those who did. I always wondered what was going through their heads. I used to think, "Man, they didn't do anything, so why are they so happy?" I was that guy now.

1 think it goes without explanation, what a person feels like once you've been there. But I was there. I was a part of the team. I felt that I had helped contribute to the win. I had shed the same blood, sweat, and tears with the rest of my teammates. I was not a scholarship player. I was not a starter. I am Alex Meacham, and I was a walk-on.

"We're number one, we're number one." This is a cheer that in a normal situation I would welcome, but that day it sounded like someone scraping their finger nails down a chalkboard. Taunting, and teasing, "We're number one, we're number one." I had wished that it were over. I had wished that we had some fans, especially there. It was Alaska, there was three inches of snow on the ground, and it was freezing. It seemed especially cold in there because we had no fans, everybody was cheering for Duke and the place was filled to capacity. This was a big deal because anyone who knows anything about basketball knows that Duke is one of the winningest programs in college basketball history. And for us to come all the way to the Great Alaska Shootout and have the crowd on their side was like them having a sixth man on the court.

I was thinking to myself, we weren't even supposed to be here. Especially after just two nights before our show- down with Duke when we barely snuck past Southern Utah, a team that we should have easily beaten. Our Coach Bob Huggins was so mad that he pulled out all five starters and replaced them with the five players on the bench. I was one of the five on the bench.

Usually 1 was ready for an opportunity like that one, but that night wasn't the night. I had the flu. I couldn't breathe. My eyes were watering, and it felt like I had cotton stuck up my nose. I felt like that old guy who comes to the park to play with the kids, and after a fastbreak he's bent over calling a timeout. One of the team doctors looked at me and asked me how did I feel, and I said, "Like I'm 80 years old."

I was sitting there thinking that there was no way in the world I would be able to get out there and run up and down the court. However, I was predicting a blowout, and I was getting mentally prepared for the end of the game. But when coach called my name to go in the beginning of the first half, I jumped up as if someone had set my seat on fire. How would you tell one of the winningest coaches in the nation that you couldn't go into the game because you had the sniffles?

When I stepped on the court, something took over my body. For the next eight minutes in the first half I ran up

and down the court using every last bit of energy I had, and even some that I didn't have. But from somewhere I found the strength. At one point in the game during a free throw, I was hunched over gasping for air. My body was aching.

My head was throbbing. My nose was running uncontrollably, but for some strange reason I never felt better in my life. Being in that position was one of the greatest moments I'd ever experienced.

We won the game and even though I had only contributed three points, I felt as if I had a lot to do with that win. Our goal in the Great Alaska Shootout was not just to play Duke, but to beat Duke in the championship game, and I had helped us get one step closer to our goal.

Again the next night we played bad. For the second time in two games we barely snuck by another team we should have easily beaten, Iowa State. But the past two nights didn't matter right then, because we were in the championship game, and we had reached our target.

However, I remember at that particular moment all I could think about was all of the millions of people watching at home in as much amazement as I was, to what was possibly about to happen. We were about to beat Duke, the number one team in the country. I don't remember if I actually said that out loud, but even if I did, it didn't matter because you couldn't hear anything above the chants of "We're number one, we're number one." A cheer that still seemed strange to me because we were so far away from Cameron Indoor Stadium and the amount of Duke support that filled the stands.

Standing in the huddle with only seconds left in the game and one last chance to do the impossible, I couldn't stand still. I couldn't watch Coach Huggins give his last instructions to a play I had seen us execute a hundred times in practice. I didn't know if it would work. But I had seen it work before. I had seen Duke use it to beat Kentucky and go on to win a national championship. Think about the irony. Us using a play against Duke that they executed to perfection. I took a deep breath and really began to doubt that it would work.

I was shaking. My palms were sweaty. If someone had asked me if I were all right, I would have had to say no. I didn't feel sick, even though I had been suffering from the flu for the last couple days. I couldn't sit down and I didn't want to stand up for fear that I might have lost my balance. There were only 3 seconds on the clock, and there was one last chance for a big play.

The whistle blew. It was time. Ryan ("Fletch") Fletcher, our starting forward, like his days as a high school quarterback, dropped back and threw the ball. The ball was in the air, and then it happened.

Have you ever been watching a movie and it comes to a suspenseful scene and everything is in slow motion? You know the scene that I am talking about, the one where everything slows down to a crawl, and only one isolated sound is heard. No crowd, no screams, just the pounding of your heart. It was like being trapped in a vacuum. It became silent. So silent that I thought the crowd could hear the thoughts that I was so deeply caught in.

My thoughts carried me back to the first time I ever felt this much excitement. It was October and it should have been getting colder around that time, but on that day I remember it was unusually hot. I remember sitting in the locker room wondering what it was going to be like, being part of a team again. I remember something hitting me square in the chest; it was a feeling of excitement. I was a part of Midnight Madness at the University of Cincinnati. Not as a fan, which I had been for so many years, but as a player. I still remember the whole thing like it was yesterday. When Midnight Madness was over I almost tackled my dad. I couldn't just hug him, because the event itself had come and gone but not the excitement that still ran through my body.

That was the same excitement that I was feeling during that moment of the Duke game. I was way up in Alaska, so who would I run to this time, who would I hug? I thought to myself that maybe I was jumping the gun, the game wasn't over yet. The ball, just like myself, had a lot of court left to travel before its destination, and the final buzzer sounded.

I got real nervous watching our starting center, Kenyon Martin, catch the pass from Fletch. Not so much for Kenyon and the game, but for me! Through all the struggles, disappointments, and sleepless nights, I had made it. And while I was nervous on the inside, there was a sense of calm on the outside. I felt comfortable. I felt like I belonged.

Growing up, I'd heard the biblical story about a man who walked on water. Not until this moment did I realize how good that must have felt. That grand feeling of accomplishing something no one thought you could do. Meeting, greeting, and defeating the odds.

And just as quickly as I had slipped into my trance I was awakened with a bang, when Kenyon with his long body passed the ball with the grace of a ballerina to Melvin Levett. Without sounding like a cliche, it was poetry in motion when Melvin took off his jersey and showed the world he had wings. Melvin soared through the air and brought us back to life with a thunderous dunk. There was still one second left, but the game was really over.

The buzzer sounded, and that was it.

Taking in the moment, I had time to think about how long my journey had been. I use to take walking for granted; Think about it, some people are not even able to walk. I never knew where my walk would take me, or where I might end up, or that this walk would be my walk of a lifetime.

CHAPTER 2

MOON WALK

To understand just how much it meant for me, a walk- on, to make the University of Cincinnati Bearcat team, I must take you back to the beginning, a physical and mental rewind of how and why I did what I did.

It has always been a practice of mine to conduct what I refer to as "The Alex Assessment" whenever I take on a major challenge in life. Simply put, I give myself a reality check to decide whether the challenge I am about to encounter outweighs the risks involved. If the challenge measures up, it's no looking back, no regrets. If not, it is often a sign that maybe I need to give the challenge a little more thought.

As I have found out through the years, when something's right, you just know it. Some of the influential adults in my life use to say, "You gotta crawl before you walk." I soon discovered just how right they were.

From my days as a youth, playing basketball has always been a passion of mine. I quickly bonded to the game and could not be pulled away from it. While I tried other sports such as baseball, even soccer, I quickly found out nothing measured up to taking a ball, finding a hoop, and losing myself on the court. Even to this day, whenever I need to get away from whatever's bothering me, I'll find the closest court available and remain there for hours.

Playing basketball has always been an offbeat way of expressing myself. Whenever I would get to a court, I always felt like it was my time to shine. I was never arrogant, nor did I show anyone up in particular. I would simply display an inner confidence that can sometimes get lost along the way. It's funny, but I've found that overcoming obstacles is often about finding out where you fit. When I was playing basketball, I always felt like I belonged.

Even when I recall my days as a member of my youth team, Bon-Pad, there were always obstacles to overcome. My coach back then, Willie C. Jackson, use to continually challenge me to be the best that I could be. He always used humor to help ease the tension, like calling me "Buckethead" whenever I would make a mistake. It was his way of getting the point across, but at the same time, keeping the game fun. Just like many others in my day, I thought basketball was all about no-look passes and ball handling wizardry. Quickly I learned that looking good did not always translate into being good. Coach Jackson was one of the first people to teach me that.

While I've always felt that I was a fairly decent ball player, somehow I was certain there was a better player inside of me. Not some horror movie freak show type, but an inner presence that kept pushing me to get better. One day I was certain the two would meet. "Decent" would become "Destined."

My days playing for Bon-Pad prepared me well for the challenges ahead. At times I was not so sure that playing against people two or three years older was beneficial. Later I found out that the stronger the competition, the greater the desire to get better. And better meant more than just thinking about it. Before I knew it I would be thrown into a world I knew very little about. A world that stressed fundamental excellence, disciplined work habits, and scheduled study times. I also discovered a process I refer to as "mental edging;" that is, knowing the game, not just playing the game.

As a seventh grader, I attended Doherty Middle School, a branch of the Seven Hills School system. Seven Hills is built on academic excellence. There, basketball was important, but the ability to spell it was the true focus. In a moment of contemplation, I realized that another "Alex Assessment" was not far away.

My coaches at Doherty, Tom Betts and Ed Wiseman, constantly told me that I had all the talent in the world. But they also emphasized that talent alone was a lost gift without knowing the basic fundamentals of the game. Sometimes I felt as if Coach Jackson, Coach Betts, and Coach Wiseman were related. Now that I think about it, they were, from a basketball perspective.

Until this point, I had always relied on my talent alone. Who needs fundamentals, so I thought, when you can pass or shoot like me? Not to brag, but even back then I had a great shot and a soft touch from the outside. I remember a time when I received a resounding applause for sinking three pointers at halftime of a Cincinnati game. Ironic huh? And not bad for a thirteen-year old ball boy, who idolized the sweet touch of prolific NBA guard, Glen Rice.

In seventh grade, I played on the eighth grade team. I was doing pretty well, and soon began to understand the need to know more about the game. The coaches were right. Having the fundamentals of the game did separate goodness from greatness. It all came down to how hard I wanted to work; and a few other things that I'll talk about later. While there's more to the game than fundamentals, a strong fundamental base is truly the cornerstone to a solid basketball foundation.

Both coach Betts and Wiseman began to notice my progress. They even named a drill after me. Unsurprisingly it became known as the "Alex Drill." I would take the ball, wrap it around both legs, and then go through each leg individually. I conducted the drill with such speed and accuracy, that I left my name on it. Even today, when I go back and attend summer basketball camps at Seven Hills, many people refer to that particular drill as "The Alex Drill." Their acknowledgment is a compliment I'll always treasure.

Even though I was doing well, I wanted to get better. Something inside of me was just not satisfied. My ambition soon translated into more practice time, more drills, more learning. I recall one day when Coach Betts showed our team a video of two men called the Lehmann Brothers. One half of this instructional piece featured George Lehmann conducting the techniques of shooting. It seemed like he must have shot 300 times without missing a single shot. It was incredible as well as inspirational. The other half of the video showed George's brother, Austin, demonstrating the proper techniques for ball handling. While I loved shooting, ball handling was my passion.

The video took my interest in getting better to another level. It also gave me a deeper appreciation for Coach Betts, who, I feel, was one of the great teachers of the game. He knew how to get you to understand, be it a video, or something he would say. Whenever Coach Betts was through I always had a lull understanding of what I needed to do. While I also have great respect for Coach Wiseman, I never really got to play for him. He mainly coached the seventh graders, and I had stepped up a year. Coach Wiseman even kidded me saying, "If you had played for me in seventh grade, you would be starting for Bob Huggins."

Remember when I said I felt the need for an "Alex Assessment" at the beginning of Doherty School? Well assessment time came a little sooner than I had anticipated. At Seven Hills High School, making the grade was not an option. You either kept up or got out. Quietly, but in no way proud, I decided to leave.

It was not that I felt inferior, but I knew that at this point in my life, I was simply not on a level to keep up. My parents were both educators, and in my household there was a strong sense of pride in achieving good grades. After a brief debate, my parents and I decided that I should try another school for my high school years. The choice was Purcell Marian.

At Purcell I was excited, but fitting in became a little awkward. Even back then, and to this day, I'm somewhat of a free spirit. I'm a person who makes his own path instead of following someone else's. At Purcell, as was the case at Seven Hills, the path was already mapped out, the trees cut. With that in mind, I knew another assessment would not be far off.

Attending school at Purcell was an adjustment, but playing basketball was an even greater challenge. At this stage in my life problems seemed like a bad cold. They just wouldn't go away.

Although I made varsity as a sophomore and played well, Coach Mike Gergen and I often disagreed. It seemed no matter what I did, it was never enough! I just couldn't bring myself to adjust to the yelling and screaming. Don't get me wrong. I have always believed that if I messed up I deserved to hear about it. It was just the manner in which it was delivered that gave me problems.

One day, while practicing for a big game, Coach Gergen was all over me. I tried to ignore him, listening only to what I thought was important. It just didn't work. Without a second thought, I tossed my practice jersey on the floor and walked away. Of all the walks in my life, this is one I'm probably the least proud of. I suppose if I would have known that one day I'd be playing for such a demanding and vocal coach as Bob Huggins, I might have stuck it out, if only to prepare my ears for what was to come.

In an offbeat way, Coach Gergen served as my college prep class for "Huggins 101." And although we rarely saw eye-to-eye, I gained a lot of respect for Coach Gergen and what he tried to accomplish. Nevertheless, I'd made my decision to leave Purcell, and quite frankly, I wasn't sure what I'd do next. With my head spinning and my confidence wrecked, I decided once again to transfer to another school. This time I'd either make it, or walk completely away from the game I loved.

Through my perils, I was beginning to understand something. Life was not one big step, but a series of small ones. Each step was critical to the journey. If nothing else, I understood that I must adapt to certain situations. But man was I tested!

Now faced with my third "Alex Assessment" in as many years, it was time to settle down. It was time to find a home and pursue my dream of playing high school basketball.

After some brief research and problem solving, I decided to attend Roger Bacon High School. With my window of opportunity closing fast, I honestly felt this was my best shot, from every angle.

When I arrived at "Bacon," as the students called it, I somehow brought a reputation for being a pretty good ball player. One day while I was sitting in the cafeteria, a guy came over to me and said, "I heard you're pretty good. We'll see how good you are tonight." That's all he said, and that was all I needed to hear. Stepping up to a challenge was like music to my ears. The day couldn't go fast enough.

As I arrived at open-gym after classes, I was fully prepared. It was my time to show the new coach, Bill Brewer, and the rest of Roger Bacon, just what I was made of. What made it even more challenging was the fact that most of last year's starters were back at Bacon. Coach Brewer had already informed me that making the team would be a difficult task. Nevertheless, challenges are what made me tick.

Dressed for the occasion in my traditional knee high socks and black Air Jordans, I was ready to fly. The guy who challenged me in the cafeteria was also there. The scene could not have been better.

Within the first minutes of the game, I saw my opportunity. A statement was about to be made. I saw a shot go up. I took off with a running start and leaped over the kid who had shared with me his cafeteria wisdom. Grabbing the rebound, I dribbled the length of the court and drove in for an easy lay-up. Much to my surprise, almost everyone seemed frozen in time, everyone except me. With all eyes glaring in my direction, I quietly heard the cafeteria historian say, "Damn." From that point on I knew I was in. I found out later that the cafeteria trash talker was none other than Mitch Perdrix, the best player Bacon had at the time. He and I later became good friends. To this day we still laugh about our classic meeting.

I was thrilled that I had made the team. It seemed as if the cold that had stopped me up for years was finally cured. At the first game, I was the leading scorer, and by the second and third game I had a reputation in the league as an offensive threat. But the fourth game was the one I was really waiting for.

That fourth game was against Purcell Marian. We were in the second of three practice sessions, and my mind was totally focused on revenge. I walked into the gym for the final practice, and Coach Brewer came over to talk to me. In a strange, expressionless manner, he said, "You can't play tomorrow." I knew why.

I was struggling in algebra, and as soon as I heard his words, I knew I had failed. I was ineligible! I couldn't believe it was happening again.

To make matters worse, all the transferring from one school to another had come back to haunt me. Not only was I ineligible for the remainder of my junior year, but my senior year was lost as well. My dreams of high school stardom had now become a nightmare of missed opportunities.

After some tears over all the chances I'd blown, I realized that regardless of the situation, I had to regroup. But basketball? Basketball was about to become a vision of the past, a faded possibility lost in my personal mirror of indecision. The most important thing now was graduating from high school and moving on to college. At least that's what I thought.

Following a brief recovery, I got very active in school. Finding a gym was not the only important thing any more. I discovered there was more to me that simply being a good basketball player.

I got involved in several student activities, even broadcasting the school basketball games. True enough, it was difficult, but life is a series of steps. Even through adversity, you've got to find the strength to walk on. I remember someone telling me, "Good things often come out of bad situations." At the time it was hard for me to understand how. Not until later would the saying make sense. Only by then, I would be walking to the beat of a different drum.

At the University of Cincinnati, I took an interest in student affairs. After all, since basketball was a ghost of the past, I had to keep busy. Problem was, this ghost was not about to go away. I tried a variety of things, but somehow basketball kept coming to the forefront. My friend and former nemesis, Mitch Perdrix, was off playing basketball for Northern Kentucky University. Sometimes I would go over and watch him play. In spite of all my disappointments, the fire still burned. I still had a passion for the game. It also didn't help that an inner voice kept saying, "Man you cheated yourself, and now, you'll never know."

After weeks of self-debate, I decided I would begin to play again. If nothing else, I wanted to see if I still had it. I began to work out, going back to Roger Bacon to regain my shooting touch. Even after some downtime, I found I still had it. I guess my former coaches were right again. The fundamentals of the game will carry you through just about anything; although I am not so sure they had my situation in mind when they said it.

One day while shooting around at Roger Bacon, I encountered my former gym teacher, Dan Starkey. He knew my history, but his appearance was like something out of the Twilight Zone. Only thing missing was the music. Without me saying anything he said, "You know Alex, you should try out for the Bearcats."

Startled for a moment, I simply replied, "I'm letting basketball go. I'll just play for fun." As he walked away, he said something I will never forget. "You'll regret it if you don't try." Then he went away. Almost instantly, that small spark became a flame. I didn't react immediately, but I knew another "Alex Assessment" was closing in.

After several pick-up games, my skills got better and better. I dominated at every open gym, but I wasn't so sure I could hold my own at the Division-I level. Cincinnati was one of the best programs in country. In order to be there, you had to be one of the best players in the country. Regardless of my fear, the fire was burning out of control. The desire to play again had now resurfaced. As crazy as it was, I had to find out if I could make it.

I didn't want to just go in "cold turkey," so I decided I would get a feel for what the players, the atmosphere, and most importantly, head coach Bob Huggins was like. Little did I know, Huggins' reputation as a no-nonsense coach was the least intimidating thing about the man. Encountering him personally was a nightmare all to itself.

As I got to know some of the coaching staff, in particular former assistant coach, Larry Harrison, I explained to them what I had in mind. Coach Harrison advised me to ponder the situation for a few days then return with a decision. While sharing my thoughts with the assistant coaches and a few internal people went well, taking my vision to Huggins was an entirely different story.

After running some pick-up games with a few members of the team, I had survived my first test. I wasn't overwhelmingly great, but I knew if I worked hard, I had a chance. It just so happened that before I could get off the court, Huggins came over to me.

He'd heard through our academic advisor, Jim Burbridge, what I had in mind. With his classic stare and surprisingly soft voice, he told me to get NCAA clearance and a physical, and get back to him. That's all he said, and for me, that was more than enough.

CHAPTER 3

WALK IN THE PARK

When I reflect back to where my passion for the game of basketball developed, three moments come to mind.

First, were my youthful beginnings as a member of Bon- Pad which was my first exposure to organized basketball.

Second, and probably most significant, were my sibling rivalries with my brother, Tony. Tony was the consummate point guard and there was nothing more I desired than to play with the court savvy that he did. Although our personalities were as different as night and day, me outspoken, him reserved, there was a common bond that seems inspirational for almost every young boy. I wanted to be like him. I wanted to shoot like him, dribble like him. Even more importantly, at least at the time, I wanted to beat him. It didn't matter the game, "One-on-One," "HORSE," even "21," I just wanted to win, despite an age difference of seven years.

While I knew my work was cut out for me, a certain passion to excel was born. For me, a win over Tony would be the equivalent to beating Michael Jordan in a backyard game of 21. It was a desire that would challenge me throughout all my early years.

Third, and equally inspiring, were my days of watching and playing "street-ball." I suppose you could say that playing in the parks served as an unofficial breeding ground for many of the great players, both past and present. While organized basketball is the foundation for fundamentals, the street-game is also a necessary component. Without it, very few players could have propelled themselves to the next level, be it, high school, college, even the NBA.

No matter where you go, the street-ball code of survival remains the same. Win and you keep playing, lose and you sit. At my neighborhood court, there were no exceptions. On a crowded day, a loss could seem like a lifetime sentence.

Although there were hundreds of outdoor courts in the city I could have gone to, the place where I played was called "Sugar 'n Spice." It sat down in a valley surrounded by trees, and each day the best players from around the area would assemble to showcase their skills. In a sense it served as the outdoor arena for any basketball player who wanted to play, thought he could play, or quickly found out he couldn't play. In street-ball, making the cut is a daily occurrence.

While I was too young to participate during my early years, several buddies and I would make the daily trek to watch the games. Each afternoon we would trample through the woods, cutting through a nearby golf course along the way. Although we knew we couldn't play, we always went with the anticipation that one day we might get drafted for the big show. That dream day took years to happen, but it never discouraged us from looking, and learning. And despite the odds, we always came prepared with a ball in our hands. Sometimes we would sneak in a shot when the older guys weren't looking. But most of the time we were there to observe and admire the self-proclaimed "street-ball legends" from afar. Day after day they never disappointed us.

It was unbelievable, but these guys would go at it all day. And the majority of their passion was driven by their intense iove for the game. Every now and then a scuffle would break out, but most of the time it never amounted to more than a few choice words, some animated finger pointing, and a ball being thrown in the woods. Nowadays you hear people talk about "trash-talking" and "taunting" as if it's some newly discovered violation of the game. Fact is, it's just one of the many elements of the street-game. Always has been. Always will be.

Anyone who has played in the streets knows that those who speak the loudest often get the most attention. While Sugar 'n Spice had numerous legends, one in particular still lives on today. His name, at least on stage, was "Money Station." And as he put it, he came with one agenda in mind, to make daily "deposits" and ""withdrawals."

I can remember watching him and admiring how good he was. But his narration of the game; all done while he played, was even better. Often he'd come down the court, dribble through traffic, shoot and holler, "Money in the bank," as the ball sank through the net. Even Muhammad Ali's boastful expressions had little on "Money Station." To this day if you mention his name, many of the guys who played at "Sugar 'n Spice" will smile. "Money Station" was just one of several guys who made "trash-talking" a true art form.

As I grew older, I began to understand the "street- game," both good and bad. One of the good things I picked up was the toughness it took to survive on a daily basis. In the street game, if you backed down, you were likely never to get up again. I also admired how some guys could speak volumes without ever saying a word. My brother, Tony, was one of those guys. Quiet and unassuming, yet inherently tough with a great understanding of the game. He never bought into the verbal wars of "Money Station."

Tony was a true point guard. A John Stockton of his time with a great shot and uncanny basketball savvy. To no surprise, out of everyone I isolated, he was the one I wanted to pattern my game after.

With my brother fueling my passion for the game, one thing quickly became apparent. In order to be considered the best, you've got to beat the best. No shortcuts. No Harlem Globetrotter theatrics. Just win. And for me, the only victory that would suffice was beating Tony.

Our dad had erected a small court in the backyard of our home and that is where my challenge to upset Tony began. Daily we'd play. Daily I'd lose. But despite my defeated psyche, I never gave up. I was determined that one day, I'd leave the court with a smile, and Tony would no longer rule the 17 x 12 concrete home court. It took me a while to figure everything out, but slowly I began to overcome the court's silent opponents.

I even went as far as to set up "one-on-one" duels that I referred to as "shadow hooping," the art of playing by yourself and imagining your opponent standing between you and the basket.

As I worked out my strategy, I concluded that one day the rose bushes would no longer scratch my skin or tear my shirts. I also knew that there would come a time when the porch over-hang would not reject my shot, playing the role of Shaquille O'Neal vs. a grade school die-hard. Even one day, I'd overcome the concrete cracks that sometimes cause the ball to possess a mind of its own.

Tony already knew how to overcome those obstacles. So in order to beat Tony, I had to be mentally, as well as physically, prepared.

Eventually Tony taught me some of the finer points of the game. It was never enough to beat him, but more than enough to hold my own with my neighborhood buddies. I even learned how to take a charge, although I later found out it's not a good idea for street-ball.

When Tony wasn't available, my buddies and I would play all day, recreating our favorite players' moves, while developing some new ones of our own. For us, weather was never a factor. I guess we were “Postal-kids,” playing through the rain, the sleet, and the snow. Once you develop a passion for something, obstacles become motivation.

I recall one day in the dead of winter, a friend and I decided that we wanted to play a game of “one-on-one.” For us, it didn’t matter that is was cold outside, and that our backyard court was covered with ice. Regardless of the elements we forged ahead with shovels, even hot water; which eventually turned back into ice. We played the game anyway. It didn’t last long, but we’d accomplished what we set out to do. And to my surprise that particular day would prove crucial to my determination to become a Bearcat.

I found out through ‘trial and error” that if there’s something you want, you have to willing, and able, to adapt. From there it’s simply a case of how bad you want it.

Throughout my two years as a walk-on, I often reflected back to my days on the concrete courts. Some things never say “Goodbye,” but simply “So-long”.

“So-long” until you need them to push you to excel. “So-long” until you have to call upon the brash statements of a “Money Station” to prove your worthiness. Even “So- long” until memorable battles with your older brother drive you over unbelievable odds. If nothing else, the backyard battles and the Sugar ‘n Spice showdowns taught me about the line of separation, that thin line between a challenge and a victory.

For me to become a member of the Cincinnati Bearcats, and to eventually dethrone my brother, the challenge was to never give up. My victory, as it was in both cases, would come only after suffering several defeats. Little did I know, until years later, that a long walk in the park would one day serve as my pathway to a walk of a lifetime.

CHAPTER 4

FEET DON'T FAIL ME NOW

Basketball is a combination of both mental and physical things. Although this holds true for around ninety-nine percent of the participants, my case as a walk-on was slightly different.

Once again I began to think about just where I was, and what I was trying to accomplish by being a walk-on. I found that "hopeful" would become a key word in my vocabulary. Not just hopeful that I could compete and eventually make the team, but also hopeful that in doing so I would earn the respect and support of my teammates, coaches, and fans. In order to make everything come together, I needed an edge. I needed something, or someone, who could help me achieve above and beyond even my own expectations. From this point forward, pencil in my number one fan and mentor, Jerome Gray.

After a strenuous workout at the Shoemaker Center, one day, I was walking back to my car. I was in deep thought about the impossible goal I was trying to reach. I looked up briefly, and crossing my path was a familiar face. It was Jerome. I hadn't seen him in three years. We talked briefly and suddenly it hit me. Was he that edge I needed?

Jerome had a connection to Bearcat basketball, he was a former walk-on! He was someone who could help me survive my first hurdle, the Bearcats' brutal conditioning program.

For Jerome, helping me was his way of giving back. Once I explained to him what I wanted to accomplish he took me step by step through the entire walk-on process. He gave me words of encouragement, but he also created self- generated workouts that proved to be important to my success. It's a funny thing when preparation meets opportunity, good things often occur. This was definitely the case for how Jerome and I met.

Although I knew who Jerome was, our paths rarely crossed prior to my decision to become a walk-on. But even before we met, I'd been made aware of Jerome's nickname, "J-Fresh" on several occasions. For Jerome popularity was clearly not a problem. Call it fate. Label it destiny. In some strange way it seemed that Jerome and I were drawn together by one common interest: Basketball at the University of Cincinnati. Once again I entered my own Twilight Zone. This time I decided not to question it. I simply went along and took it as a sign that I was headed in the right direction.

From day one Jerome instilled in me that walking on would not be an easy task. In the same breath, he said that if I were willing to put everything on the line, my chances of making the team were better than average. I decided to go for it, and the grueling workout process began.

Each day, he and I would meet after classes and go through conditioning. Not just any conditioning, but conditioning, Bearcat style. Sometimes we would go back to Seven Hills School for some additional workouts. Former Seven Hills coach and current athletic director, Duke Snyder, would sometimes let us in the school for some late night workouts. At times I wondered if it was all worth it, but I kept focused. For once in my life, I was not going to blow an opportunity based on feelings alone.

As the days leading up to "Bearcat conditioning" went by, the workout sessions with Jerome got more intense. I would work on a variety of shooting drills, and then he and I would play one-on-one until late in the evening. When the physical portion of learning the game was over, Jerome would talk to me about what to expect on the day of reckoning. Jerome had great knowledge of the game, and I was taking in everything he said.

We talked endlessly about the role of a walk-on and about earning the respect of the highly touted players who, unlike me, were recruited for a reason. I remember one night Jerome and I had a "heart-to-heart" talk over chicken wings at a local restaurant. The session lasted until the wee hours of the morning. At times it seemed as if both of us were trying to make the team. At that moment, I knew I'd found the edge I was looking for.

With my preparation going well, I decided to inform a select number of people about what I was trying to accomplish. Besides my family, only Jerome and my roommate, Sam, knew at this time. Pd learned through watching my older brother that a silent walk often speaks louder than an announced one. Besides, if I fell short of my goal, I would not have to suffer the "I told you so's." I was obviously protecting myself from potential hurt.

While Jerome prepared me well on all fronts, I knew he would not be there when the "real" conditioning began. He would also not be there at my first meeting with Coach Huggins. I had to prepare myself mentally to talk to Huggins, but how?

As 1 walked into the Men's Basketball Office, I felt as if I'd landed on some desert island. I was not scared necessarily, but I just wasn't sure where to find the resources to make the most of this conversation. Coach Huggins was not only an intimidating man, but he was also very busy. If there was one thing I didn't want to do, it was waste his time.

The night before I'd prepared myself with some 3x5 note cards. Nothing elaborate, but just some points of reference in case I began to babble. I've found through the years that being prepared is more than a Boy Scout battle cry. It's an essential part of life.

Waiting for Coach Huggins to arrive was probably the worst. All kinds of negatives ran through my mind. What if he didn't like me? Will he be in a bad mood? What if he asked me something I didn't know? I even considered coming back at another time; as if my thoughts would change at a later date. Before I could muster up the nerve to reconsider, he arrived.

Without saying much, he motioned for me to follow him into his office. The time was now, and backing out was not an option. As I walked in, the setting was much different from I had anticipated. His office, although large in size, had a somewhat eerie lighting scheme. It's hard to describe but the lights seemed very, very dim. I tried not to look intimidated, but I was. Was this to be yet another Twilight

Zone for me? As he sat behind his desk, and I sank into an adjacent leather chair, I couldn't help but notice the larger- than-life image of the man.

Directly behind me was an autographed picture of Huggins arm-in-arm with Michael Jordan. For some odd reason it was comforting to know that "His Aimess" was smiling upon me. Alongside the Jordan portrait was a picture of former Bearcats standout, Nick Van Exel, now with the Denver Nuggets. Meeting Huggins was like meeting God himself. I thought to myself, Oh Lord, not now.

After a brief session of daydreaming, I focused in on what I'd come for. I told Coach Huggins about how I wanted to try and make the team, and how I had been preparing myself to do so. I even mentioned that I might be helpful to the team, preparing recruited guards like Michael Horton and Shawn Myrick for upcoming opponents. I wasn't sure he was buying into my theory, but he didn't look disinterested.

After my brief sales pitch, I waited for his response. I wasn't sure what he'd say, but to be honest, I expected the worst. For years, I'd seen the man in his intimidating sideline theatrics, arms wailing, scowling face, and I tried to prepare to experience it first-hand.

Much to my surprise, I didn't encounter it. Coach Huggins simply informed me of some additional preparation I needed, both physically and academically. That was it. No cuss words, no finger in my face, none of that. Had I read the man wrong, or was he setting me up? At the time, it really didn't matter. I'd made it through, so far.

As I walked out of his office, I was thrilled. He hadn't said, yes I would make it, but he hadn't said no I couldn't. I felt like it was up to me. The passion and desire I had would have to be my ace-in-the-hole. Coach Huggins was the dealer and I was the player. No bluffs. No cards on the table. I simply had to show him what I was made of. Through Jerome's belief in me, I felt it was a safe bet.

Becoming a ritual, I contacted Jerome immediately. I let him know what Huggins had said. Jerome's response was simple, "We've got to get serious now." For a moment that scared me. Weren't we already serious? As Jerome continued, I found out what he meant. His thoughts were that we needed to be more concentrated in our efforts. Translated, it simply meant, less time on the court and more mental preparation for what was to come.

I wasn't totally convinced this was the correct approach, but I had trusted Jerome, and I was convinced he would do what was right. After getting on the same page, Jerome and I spent more time talking about the situation, as opposed to trying to duplicate the environment. Later, I would see what Jerome's philosophy was. He knew there was only a certain amount of physical preparation needed. After all, I was in decent physical shape, but could I endure the mental test of "hanging-in-there" and not walking away? That was the question he knew I would have to answer.

As the "day-of-reckoning" came, I felt prepared, although I was a little unsure about how the team would receive me. When I arrived for the first meeting, to my surprise, all the guys were pretty cool. A few of them shook my hand and spoke without reserve. Even Ruben Patterson, who was one of the most highly recruited junior college players to ever come to UC, shook my hand. For a brief moment, I was beginning to feel like I belonged. But despite the welcome, I was on edge and kept my guard up.

Coach Huggins arrived shortly after I did, and I quickly realized he was not in the best of moods. Later I found out that whenever Huggins would wear his glasses to a practice, it was sign of bad things to come. His late nights of film study and preparation would often translate into long days for the team.

Coach Huggins went through his expectations for conditioning, and from that moment on we were in the hands of our then strength coach, Mickey Marrotti. Coach Marrotti was well known for his intense workouts, but his results were even more impressive. He was so good that often the bodies he transformed became known as "Bodies by Marrotti." It was a testament to the man who made the Bearcats one of the most physically dominant teams in the country.

I thought I was in decent shape, but I had no idea what it would take to endure the Bearcats tough conditioning program. The moment we stepped onto the track and began our first mile run, I knew why Jerome had drilled me so hard. Being a Bearcat, walk-on or recruit, would not be an easy task.

Running a mile is one thing. Running a timed mile is a completely different story. For whatever reason, I was not prepared for stopwatches and timed drills. Nervous already, my heart fell to my feet when Coach Marrotti informed us that we would have to run our mile under six minutes. "Did he say six or sixteen minutes?" I thought.

Unfortunately it was six. And if you didn't make it the first time, you did it again.

As we began our laps, my throat dried up quickly, and my mouth became a cotton field. My legs began to wobble as if they were unattached. I'm sure, at least for a moment, I looked like the scarecrow in the Wizard Of Oz. With my heart pounding, I thought, "What am I doing here?" I tried desperately to keep pace with guys like Ruben and Kenyon, but that was a mistake.

These guys were not only in better shape, but their long legs were a definite plus when setting a pace for themselves. My short strides only made me work harder. As we circled around for the last lap, I said, "Yes," while my body pleaded "Stop." My mind won out, but only because I couldn't harbor the thought of quitting on my first day.

With sweat pouring down my face, the mile was over. But that was only the beginning. Next up, we had to run one lap as fast as we could. While I thought it sounded easy enough, 1 had no idea this was just one of six laps that day. "No way," I thought. He's got to be kidding." He wasn't.

"No pain, no gain," I tried to remember. "This is what you wanted," I told myself. While it's obvious that I made it through, I truly don't know how. I was determined not to quit like I had in the past. This time I would not give in!

One time during these exhausting "sprint laps" I cramped up so bad I thought I was having a seizure. To my saving grace, I was not the only one in pain. Kenyon and Michael Horton were suffering too. Lucky for all of us, Coach Marrotti gave us a break. It was one of the few times I was happy to have someone else in pain besides me. I made it through the first day, but tomorrow was just around the corner. As I sat in my class the next day, I thought, "Here we go again." Eventually things got so bad that my mind would play tricks on me during class. At one point I felt as if my professor had transformed himself into Coach Marrotti. He would say something like, "Go write your thoughts on the board," and I'd sprint out of my seat. This sounds like a stretch, but several of my teammates experienced the same thoughts.

From the outdoor track, we went inside for floor work. We jumped rope and did exercises to improve footwork. We also ran what we called "22's." That meant you had to run up the court, down the court, up the court, down the court in less than 22 seconds. That's 376 feet of hardwood in 22 seconds. The catch was you had to do this ... 22 times! From that day forward, 2 + 2 never equaled 4. This exercise was brutal, and when it was over, a celebration was likely to take place.

One day while enjoying the fact that we had made it through another day of 22's, Michael Horton broke our bubble of joy. With guys laughing and smiling about their accomplishment for the day, Michael solemnly said, "You know what fellas? We've got to be back here tomorrow." It goes without saying that Michael's reality check spoiled our moment in the sun.

Last and probably most grueling was the weight room. Ever since the Huggins era the Bearcats have been known for their strenuous weight program. Often we were considered the strongest team in college basketball.

Prior to walking on, I was never a big fan of lifting weights. I knew it had a place in basketball, but how intense could it get? "I'm here for basketball, not football,"

I thought. I was wrong, but only about playing football. It's safe to say 1 was rather intimidated the first time I participated.

Our schedule was Monday, Wednesday, and Friday. Each day was intense and overloaded with the sound of clanging steel. Heavy weights, light weights, everything. One day we would do upper body, the next day lower. On the third day was full body. Coming into the UC program, I quickly found out I was a true lightweight.

After the first week, I remember continually checking to see if my limbs were still attached. Several times I thought, "This is crazy." But I stuck with it, and eventually I became proud of my accomplishments in the weight room. The girls also took notice, and that was a plus, as well.

Three weeks of running, lifting, and playing seemed like three years. But as the days went on, things got easier, as easy as they could get, considering I felt that death would be a better option than another day of conditioning. Regardless of the rubbery legs and weak stomach, I was determined not to quit. After conditioning we would often play five-on-five. With my muscles sore, my game had taken a temporary turn for the worst. Nevertheless, I didn't get discouraged, I simply pressed forward. I remember one time the team bailed out on the five-on-five games after running. Coach Huggins found out and was furious. It did not happen again!

As October 15th approached, the first day of practice, I felt as if I were ready. Jerome was still in my comer, and we continued our daily evaluations about what was going on. Now that I'd endured conditioning, it was on to my next hurdle, earning respect on the court.

In basketball one of two things happens. You either earn respect, or you get disrespected. There is no grey area for this unwritten law of the land. Thus, I was certain that making a positive statement early would help me make the team. Jerome felt otherwise.

He explained to me that the sole role of the walk-on, especially on such a talented team, was to blend in and make the rising stars shine. While I knew that Jerome would not mislead me, I had no intentions on letting the guys around me get the impression that I was soft, or had no game. I had become confident I could hold my own. On this rare occasion, I went opposite Jerome's advice, at least momentarily.

One day while going through some intense drills, one of our star players, Melvin Levett, was having a tough time with Coach Huggins. For Huggins anything short of 110% will never do. He also has no problem letting you know when your effort was not good enough. His 4ttake-no- prisoner" attitude is often reflected in the way his teams play. Nothing dirty, or illegal, just simple hard nose basketball every second you're on the court.

Melvin, a shooting guard, was a gifted athlete who had an unbelievable vertical leap and an intense upbeat demeanor to match. He was normally high strung, but with some choice words from Huggins popping in his eardrums, Melvin had become laid-back for the day. It also didn't help that a national magazine article had just placed him among the most overrated players in college basketball.

On one particular drill, Melvin and I happened to be on the same team. Melvin was open as I brought the ball down court. Instead of passing to him, I shot and missed.

While Huggins said little to me about the shot, he ripped into Melvin about not getting the rebound. Melvin turned to me, gave me a stare, and ran back down the court.

Repeating the same drill, I again decided that it was more important for me to establish myself rather than let the star have his way. Again I shot and again I missed. Huggins continued his onslaught, ripping Melvin for not hustling and following up the shot. As the intensity increased, I should have known better than to try my luck. Yet, still I did.

On the third time down, I again decided to take the shot. Only this time when I missed, Melvin retaliated. Not physically, but verbally he let me know that I was a walk- on, and walk-on's had no place among the elite. While I was not shocked that he exploded, I felt I had to stand up for myself. If nothing else, I had to inform the remaining star- studded cast that this extra would not be intimidated. In no uncertain terms, I replied to Melvin, "Oh I forgot, you're the most overrated player in the country." To make matters worse, some of our teammates overheard that statement, and laughed. I was certain that Melvin and I were headed for a fight, but it never happened. However, we did share more unkind words throughout the remainder of the day.

After practice that day, I realized that once again, Jerome had been right. I was just a walk-on with a role to play. Unfortunately, or at least for the moment, I wanted to be a star too. But the reality was that I was simply a low- priced extra on stage with stars. Although I gained some respect, showing up one of the lead characters was not the way to do it.

Melvin and I didn't speak for several days after our confrontation, but I soon learned just where I stood with the man many people referred to as "The Helicopter." During the next game, we were blowing out a team. Blowouts were a good sign that I might get some minutes. I did, but not the way I'd envisioned. With about two minutes left in the game, Melvin came over to Coach Huggins and said, "Put Alex in." Strange thing was that I was replacing him.

As the buzzer sounded for me to go in, Melvin grabbed me by the arm and said, "You better score." I was shocked, yet thrilled at the same time. I went in the game, and scored the first points of my career. From that time on, Melvin was one of my greatest supporters. He and I never talked about the incident after that, but I guess there was a silent understanding that everything was okay. It also became clear that I was both right and wrong in the way I handled it. Right because I stood up for myself. Wrong because I stepped out of my role as a walk-on.

I continued to practice hard everyday. I now knew what was important to the team. It was my role to prepare my teammates for their upcoming opponents. That was my role. That was my place on a team laced with talented athletes.

Practices were always tough, but as the year progressed, I began to fit in. I even established myself as one of the best players during "close-out" drills for the guards. Assistant coach Mick Cronin would always oversee this one-on-one drill and without bragging, I consistently beat my more heralded teammates. At times they were not thrilled about being shown up. But regardless of their personal feelings, when I got the chance, I did what I do best. I made them work in hopes that I'd make them better. After all, the opposition couldn't care less about showing you up, so why should I? Only now I did it within the context of the drill and I kept my personal feelings to myself.

A lot of things happened during my first year to test my patience. Each day I had to keep reminding myself that I had accomplished what I'd set out to do. I had become a member of the University of Cincinnati Bearcat basketball team. There was no better feeling than that.

As a walk-on, I had to make many sacrifices. I played several games in a jersey with no name on the back. I endured some rejection by Coach Huggins. I even had my temper tested by key members of Huggins' staff. True enough I was merely a walk-on, but hadn't I endured the same conditioning and drills that the recruits had? I had, and this was all a part of the sacrifice. And although it did get better, I sometimes thought my existence was purely on a game-by-game basis.

One day, while walking across campus, I was filled with negative thoughts. I ran into one of our highly recruited guards, D'Juan Baker. After some brief small talk, and a few jokes, D'Juan said something that would quiet every doubt I ever had. He looked me straight in the eye and said, "Alex you are a Bearcat now." We exchanged a ceremonial chest-bump and went our separate ways.

As I walked along campus, I began to think about the significance of D'Juan's statement. Yes, I was a Bearcat. And true enough it was a great accomplishment. But even more important was the fact that I now felt like I belonged. I now had the feeling that had escaped me throughout my high school years. The feeling of "success."

CHAPTER 5

WALKING IN SUNSHINE

How many times have you heard the saying, "There's light at the end of the tunnel?" Or have you heard, "Through adversity, strength is found."

I can recall throughout many of my most troubling times, someone would use one of these positive motivators. Early on in my life I simply nodded and thanked them for their token of support. But the truth was I never understood the point they were trying to get across. I remember thinking to myself, "Wouldn't it be easier for me to simply carry a flashlight through my tunnel of despair?" If nothing else I could avoid bumping into things along the way. As fate would have it, I'd have no such luck. Later it became apparent that the reason people say these things is because, quite frankly, they are true.

Prior to becoming a Bearcat, my road traveled was often filled with dark pathways. And even after I had "made it," there were many occasions when I was lost in a vacuum of self-doubt and misdirection. Had it not been for my early walks through those dark tunnels, I'm certain my dream to become a Bearcat would not have come to light.

What I understand about the game of basketball, and more importantly, the game of life, is that you never conquer either one, you simply get better as time goes on. As Coach Huggins puts it,

"You find a way." One summer, long before coach Huggins and I ever met, I too was challenged with having to "find a way."

It was summer vacation and my parents and I were set to enjoy the West Coast atmosphere of San Francisco, California. Yet despite the sunny skies and numerous attractions, I couldn't wait to get back home. After all, to me, summertime meant one thing. Open gym at Seven Hills School. This summer, in particular, was a great opportunity for me to make a name for myself before the next school year began. But there I was miles away from the one thing I loved most. It also didn't help that my parents had recently bought me a new pair of "Air Jordan" sneakers, and I was eager to make the transformation into "Being like Mike." After persuading my parents to leave, I was back in Cincinnati and headed to the gym. As I got there all the guys were choosing teams and making predictions about the outcome. Shortly before we began, our coach had brought along a new challenge. His name was Byron Larkin. And believe me, he was more than a challenge, he was a legend in the making. Byron was what many refer to as a prolific scorer. He would later take his talents on to Xavier University, in Cincinnati, where he became Xavier's all- time leading scorer with 2,696 points.

As we finished choosing sides, it became obvious that someone was going to have to make an attempt to guard Byron. Although he was older than I, and better, this was the challenge that brought me back home. Staring me in the face was an opportunity to go "one-on-one" with one of the best players in the city. I couldn't pass it up.

The game began and I was ready, so I thought. We went back and forth a few times, and so far, so good. Unfortunately this good feeling didn't last. In reality it became quite painful, literally.

What happen next is somewhat eerie and to this day I'm not certain as to the exact details. All I remember was Byron coming at me on a fast break, and, as I made an attempt to defend him, his foot kicked me in the knee. The next thing I heard was a pop, followed by a terrible pain! As I laid there on the floor all I could think was, "Oh no! Not now!"

With everyone surrounding me and cautioning me not to look, I knew my knee must have been in bad shape. I guess it was the fact that my bone was practically sticking through the skin. The diagnosis was a tom patella tendon, and summertime basketball had now become a broken dream. Coming up now was surgery, rehabilitation, and the challenge of surviving my first serious injury.

This is the point in my life where I developed a better appreciation for those quotes and phrases that people always seemed to share with me. One in particular became a theme I still live by today. "You never miss your water until your well runs dry." That's the one that stuck with me throughout my trying days of rehabilitation. I guess the reasoning behind it was that during rehab you often feel as if you're walking through the desert alone. And believe me, when your thirst is rarely quenched you somehow develop a true appreciation for each droplet missed along the way.

As my knee slowly regained its strength, I now began to reevaluate my approach to the game of basketball, as well as my approach to the game of life. Upon this eye-opening reflection, it became evident that on any given day, at any moment, your life can change. On the court, off the court, anywhere. And how you respond to that change determines your next step. It was time for adversity to build a better, stronger, and more energized Alex Meacham.

While injuries are a part of every sport, I don't think most athletes understand just how significant a sprained ankle or a broken leg can be in their career. Fact is, athletes are just one play away from the end of their career.

One slip, one fall, one misguided step, can place any potential star face-to-face with the hopeless reality called "finished." Even at such an early age, I understood this. What's confusing, even today, is how many athletes don't value this concept.

Often times throughout my playing days, I would see guys come into the gym both physically and mentally out of shape. Most often these were the players who suffered from a multitude of injuries. The ones who consistently spent time overcoming an injury instead of preventing one. This is not to say that being in shape will protect anyone from getting hurt, but the fact is, it can be a positive step for those who want to avoid injuries.

Be it an injury, an uncooperative teammate, or a mere lack of playing time (as it was in my case) turning negative situations around 180 degrees is essential to continuing success. For a walk-on it's an everyday occurrence.

Throughout my first year, I often questioned why I decided to become a walk-on. Was it the attention? Was it the travel? Was it an egotistical notch on my belt of achievements that drove me? While I'm certain that many in my shoes endured the blood, sweat, and tears precisely for those reasons, for me the objective was simple. "I love the game of basketball," and wanted to be a part of something that had escaped me throughout my high school years. While I knew I couldn't go back in time, I was determined to reset the clock as often as possible. But even with that mindset, a thin line between "love" and "leaving" was often drawn.

When times got tough, I began to think of how many people I represented. How many people would give anything to be a part of something so special. How many people wanted to wear a Bearcat uniform, but could only admire it from afar. How many people, for whatever reason, would never experience the awesome feeling of being called, a Cincinnati Bearcat? "How could I let them down?" How could I explain to them that I walked away from their dream, and mine, simply because of a bad day at the office? The fact was, I couldn't let them down. Even more important, I couldn't let myself down. Therefore, I continued.

"True love never dies" is another saying that seems to fit my situation. I often thought about this expression during my early days as a walk-on. Don't misunderstand me, I enjoyed being a Bearcat, but there were many days when I was bored to tears. Run. Sit the bench. Get hollered at. Sit the bench. Watch Kenyon Martin block a shot into, of all places, the bench. See Melvin sky, and watch Coach Huggins turn multi-shades of red. All this, from an inconvenient spot called, the bench.

While I knew going in, I would not be coach Huggins' No. 1 option, 1 wanted to play. I wanted to get away from the three and four game stretches where I played zero minutes. This was especially true when the games were close. There seemed to be this unbreakable cycle that left me searching for motivation and a reason to get excited. For me, when the water runs downstream, I swim upstream. If for nothing else, just to say I did it.

During one pre-game snack of apple juice and sunflower seeds, I got an idea. Before the next game I would purchase a pair of knee-high black socks and make a statement. I might not play, but I would be seen. Keep in mind that these were no ordinary socks. They were nothing like my dad might wear during a backyard shoot-a-around. These were Pele soccer-style that, at the time, were definitely against the grain. I guess you could say boredom had reached its peak and I needed to spice things up a little.

As I got dressed for the game, both Melvin and Kenyon looked at me as if I had lost it. The whole night they made fun of my Darth Vadar look. Kenyon, who laughed the most, later adopted the style, and shortly after that the entire team showed up one night looking like evil villains from Star Wars.

Although I knew I might not play during this particular game, I was determined to get noticed. And I did. Comments ranged from "outrageous" to 'frendy" as I sat there profiling my new look. Even the local television play- by-play guys noticed and gave me a little free publicity.

In fact, it probably was not the best look, but it kept me going, and eased the tension of another forty minutes on the bench. Ironically, out of this moment, darkness became the light.

While my walk-on role sometimes became part coach, part confidant, part cheerleader, I relished the opportunity to be associated with one of the best teams in the country. During my two years, we were always ranked in the top ten, and with a national ranking comes national notoriety. I mean autographs, pictures, you name it.

One day while walking to my car, a thrilled Bearcat fan approached me. This young man was not necessarily searching for the Alex Meacham highlight reel. However, he did feel compelled to seek my signature from the confines of a lowly parking lot. He explained to me that his younger brother was a huge follower of the Bearcats. Obtaining my scribble would be the highlight of his day. I gladly signed and felt chills as he walked away. When you think about it, signing a piece of paper is a little thing that does so much for a fan. It often irks me when I see athletes brush off fans and refuse to sign their name, or take part in an innocent photo opportunity. While privacy is one thing, playing without a solid fan base would likely be a humiliating experience. I personally thought it was my honor to accommodate the fans. Not because of some overgrown ego, but quite simply because it was the right thing to do.

I have found through many treks of darkness that the way you approach a challenge often dictates its outcome. Negativity is the origin of self-doubt. Quite frankly, if you think you're going to get hurt, you probably will. If you think you can't make it, you probably won't. If you focus on the dark moments, you are likely never to see the light ahead.

I can now safely say that "there's light at the end of the tunnel." But the truth is, you have to be willing to stumble along the way. You have to walk the curves, as well as the straight line. If you don't, seeing your way to the other side may leave you blind to one word. "APPRECIATION"!

CHAPTER 6
MAJOR STRIDES

You can look at being a walk-on like going to a big party. The scholarship players are the guests who have been invited. The walk-on is someone who heard about the party, thought it sounded pretty cool, and just decided to show up. The first thing you have to do when you decide to go to the party is put your ego in check, and leave it at the front door.

If I did have an ego problem when I first became a walk-on at Cincinnati, it wasn't a matter of me leaving my ego at the front door. My ego was quickly tossed out for me the minute I walked in the door.

"Expecting the unexpected" is a motto that every walk- on lives by. Even though this statement is larger than life, it still caught me off guard.

It was the summer before I first walked on the team, and we were having an open gym at the Shoemaker Center. "Open gym" was a term I never suspected to be taken so literally. Sure it was open, but only to current and past Bearcat players, such as Danny Fortson of the Boston Celtics, Corey Blount of the Phoenix Suns, and former great Tarrance Gibson.

On this particular day five familiar but unwelcome faces from across town showed up. They decided to try out our "open door" policy.

For those who don't know, Cincinnati and Xavier have one of the most heated rivalries in college basketball. What makes it so special is the schools are separated by only a couple of blocks. Each year the historic battle earns its title, the Crosstown Shootout.

It was like a scene out of an old western movie. Nobody said a word. There was a long, uncomfortable silence, and a court full of dead stares. I imagined that at any time a dust cloud and some tumble weed would come rolling by, as we waited for the clock to strike high noon. The clock never struck, but it was like Mills Lane himself came to the middle of the court and said, "Let's get it on." And on it was.

I was on the team who had just won the last game, so it was our right to stay on the floor. Xavier players Torraye Braggs, Gary Lumpkin, Lenny Brown, Reggie Butler, and James Posey stepped up to play, and we got whooped.

Xavier played like it was their home court. It was so bad that we got chewed out by Tarrance. "No one should ever come into your house and beat you," he shouted as he kicked the chairs. He then grabbed Melvin Levett by the shirt and said, "If this would have happened back when I was playing, they wouldn't have left here alive."

The next game was for real. It was "ON." There was no love between the two teams, just all out war! There was so much trash talking going on that even the playground legend, Money Station, might have closed the bank early.

Over the next couple of games, the Cats brought victory back to the pride land. When both teams finally got tired, we separated, and again that eerie silence hung over us. Finally, James Posey, who now plays for the Denver Nuggets, said, "When ya'll come over to our house, ya'll gonna get dealt with just like you did here." And then they left, silently, the same way they came in through our front door.

I wasn't even officially on the Bearcat team yet, but it was at that moment when I got my first lesson on what it really meant to be a Cincinnati Bearcat.

As time ticked closer to the execution of my goal I still had not told anyone about my future plans except for my mom, dad, and my older brother. Like 1 said before, I believe in silence and letting my actions speak for me.

However, one particular night, I decided to share my secret with one of my really good friends Damon Keese. I have known Damon since grade school, and because of our time together I considered him to be one of my best friends.

It was a Thursday night and Damon and I had decided to check out one of Covington, Kentucky's night spots, The Waterfront. Neither of us was really in the clubbing mood, so we decided to sit out on the patio and talk.

We sat there for a long time and dove into many different topics and conversations. When it seemed as if there was nothing left to talk about, I asked Damon., "What do you want to do with your life right now?" He just sat there with an inquisitive look on his face and peered up at the stars. After about a minute or two of careful pondering he said, "I don't know."

I started laughing. I was laughing because the scholarly look he had on his face, while he was pondering the question, would have told you that he was coming up with a cure for some disease. I guess Damon also found the situation amusing, and also joined in my laughter.

After a few left-over laughs, I said to Damon, "I figured out what I want to do. At least for now." And that is when I unveiled my master plan, "I think I am going to try and walk on to the University of Cincinnati basketball team."

Damon had the look of the proud father on his face. It was at that moment he told me something I'll never forget. He said. "I am going to be the first person to sport an Alex Meacham Jersey."

1 remember thinking about that night while I was hunched over gasping for air one day during pre-season conditioning . I was thinking about how good it would feel to wear a Bearcat jersey with my name on it.

Levett, number twenty-one. Patterson, number twenty- three, or Martin number four. Those were the names and numbers proudly worn on the backs of my fellow teammates. But who was number forty-one?

This was a question that I had to ask myself. The red letters on my back, which to me symbolized the Bearcat blood that ran through my body, were nowhere to be seen on my jersey. I felt like the lone rebel without a name and a cause.

For some people not having a name on the back of then- jersey wouldn't seem like such a big thing. But to me, it was everything.

Sometimes the experience of being a walk-on took away a little of my pride and a lot of my spirit. At the mid-point of my first season I felt that it was time I got those things back. Not because anyone owed it to me, but because I had earned it.

People began to ask me when I was going to get my name on the back of my jersey. The question became a sore that wouldn't heal. Walk-ons don't ask questions, but I had to because that's what my heart was telling me.

I was at practice one afternoon and Frank Jessie, an administrative assistant for the basketball team, came up to me and said, "We're going to take care of everything." Sure enough later on that same day one of the managers asked me for the correct spelling of my name.

The first of my major strides came along the next home game when the announcer said, "Herrrrrrree come the Cats." The question was answered. Thirteen thousand one hundred seventy six fans now knew that No. 41 was Alex Meacham.

The name on the back of my jersey gave me a sense of pride, but it also gave me an identity.

Now that it's all over, and I think about all those home games, it gives me the chills. I get the chills because I close my eyes and can still hear the fans chanting my name.

Words cannot describe that feeling. That feeling was something that I never thought about while I was playing. I knew that if I listened to what the fans were saying, I might have been swept into the rafters of the Shoemaker Center along with the chants.

Before the season got under way, I thought to myself, "I'll probably get into a couple games and maybe some people will cheer for me." I never dreamed that those cheers would escalate like they did.

I don't remember exactly who we were playing. I don't remember how much time was on the clock, or how many points we were beating the team by. I do remember hearing a slow moaning noise that sounded like a generator getting warmed up. "Aaaallllleexx, Aaaallllleexx."

The noise was real faint. I remember that the chant had started somewhere over in the student section.

"Aaaallllleexx, Aaaallllleexx."

That moment was nothing short of amazing. Like a pebble dropped in the water, the ripples spread and soon the chant filled the entire arena.

"Aaaallllleexx, Aaaallllleexx."

The faint whisper became a thunderous roar! I remember peering out of the comer of my eye and seeing my teammates looking around in amazement.

I was trying to act as if I didn't hear what was going on. But I had been charmed like a cobra by that hypnotic chant. I didn't feel the first pointy elbow from Kenyon Martin, but the second one woke me up and I heard him say, "Hey man, I guess it's your show now." Just as Kenyon said this, Coach Huggins motioned me to the scorers' table. The Shoemaker Center erupted! From that time on the fans never left my side. Even if the game was close and they knew I wasn't going to play, the fans never ceased to chant my name. This is something that I'll always be thankful for.

Knowing that people supported what I was doing made all of the taped ankles, sore muscles, and long practices worth while.

The biggest supporters of the official Alex Meacham fan club, however, were my family and close friends. I was away on a road trip and I had phoned home for a routine check-in with my dad. I always called to give him updates as to what was going on, and to share funny stories with him. On this particular trip there was no comedy, and things were pretty routine.

As we were saying our good-byes my dad said, "I almost forgot. You got a package in the mail from Glenn." I wasn't expecting anything from Glenn, so the contents of the package were a mystery to me.

My friend Glenn Riley is a very accomplished artist, whose drawings can be seen all around Cincinnati. Glenn has also done some freelance work for Nike and Reebok. Who knew what a package from Glenn might contain. I was exited.

When I got home from our road trip I didn't waste any time opening the package. When I tore open the box and pulled out what was inside, I was speechless.

My friend Glenn had taken time to capture me on paper. He drew a poster size cartoon of me dribbling the ball in my Bearcat uniform. He caught every last detail from my goatee down to my Air Jordans. It was magnificent. To this day, I still get emotional when I read the caption:

At age 5. all I cared about was toys, candy, and cartoons.

With Pon-Bad, I was a defensive terror.

Doherty School, seventh grade, a skinny kid with big ambitions.

Seven Hills, freshman year. While my broken leg was healing, I played on the reserve team, and I was not happy.

This was one of the few games I played while at Roger Bacon.

My brother. Tony, on a rare visit from Florida, came to the Shoe to watch me practice.

Middle School Champions. I'm No. 15, front and center.

Eight years later. Conference USA Champions. (Left to Right) Shawn Myrick, Johnny Carson, Michael Horton, Melvin Levett, Ruben Patterson, Bobby Brannen. Once again I'm in the middle.

Everyone was smiling at "Senior Night." (Left to Right) My cousin Tony and his daughter, Zoe; me; my grandmother; and Coach Huggins. This is one of the rare occasions when you will see Coach Huggins smiling in a picture!

Once again I'm leaning on my basketball mentor. Jerome Gray. Without him I may not have taken the Walk Of A Lifetime.

This is me doing what I do best. I averaged the most points per minute my senior year, giving me the nickname, " The Microwave".

Jerry Fitzgerald and I, just after our three point battle. (See Chapter 8)

Josh Pastner, the walk-on from Arizona, known as the kid who never sits down. The wannabe coach is in rare form.

This is the T-shirt that my roommate had made for me. Glenn Riley drew the picture.

When I did get in the game, I felt I needed to take advantage of every second I was in.

Senior Night. My number one supporters, my mother and father, take a walk on the court with me. I'm giving five to Kenyon Martin, while wearing the first ever pair of Air Jordans. I decided to wear them to celebrate all my years of playing basketball.

I'm focused on defense. Mom and Dad always told me to stay focused on my goals and I will achieve them.

In the beginning I thought that Melvin didn't like me. He turned out to be my biggest supporter on the team

His name is Alex Meacham. Your defensive schemes amuse him. He does not play for money, because the NCAA forbids such practices. He insists upon being a walk-on because he doesn't need your charity. And someday, when the chips are down, and things aren 't looking good for the Bearcats, they will call upon him. And he will be ready.

My mom had the picture framed, so I hung it in the bedroom of my apartment. Everyone who saw the picture was completely captivated. I remember that my roommate, Sam, was especially taken by what Glenn had done.

When Glenn sent me the picture he also sent several smaller prints of the original. Sam decided to surprise me. He took one of the prints and sent it to his mother who had it made into a T-shirt for me and my family.

I remember the day that I wore the shirt to an early morning shoot around. The first person to see my new Alex Meacham "self-promotion" was Kenyon Martin. He looked at me, shook his head, and said, "Unbelievable, this guy has his own T-shirt." I just smiled and kept shooting. Everybody on the team stopped me to read the shirt. Even some of the coaches took notice, and laughed. Later on at breakfast Melvin Levett came up to me and said, " Hey man, can you get me one?" I just smiled and kept on eating.

When I started my second season I felt like I was now a member of the team. I was wondering if the fans would still remember me, or would I just be another body filling space.

I wasn't expecting anybody to chant my name, but I was curious to see how people would respond to me.

The first home game I found out that the fans had never left. I also found out that I had fans in other cities. That is the only explanation I came up with for what happened to me in Memphis.

I liked playing against Memphis because they had a unique gym shaped like a pyramid. We were up by a large margin, which assured me an appearance in the game. I had already started the mental preparation. I had holstered up my shooting arm and put on my game face. The lone ranger was ready to ride again. All of a sudden my mental picture faded.

There were about five minutes on the clock, and people started chanting my name. This was something that never happened to me on the road. What made the situation even more peculiar was the fact that the chant started way up in the rafters of the pyramid.

I mentioned before that I tried hard never to pay attention to what the crowd was saying, but this time it was different. I began looking all around. This was a mystery that I couldn't figure out.

The situation was so puzzling because all of the die-hard Bearcat fans were sitting behind our bench. It wasn't hard to spot a group of Cincinnati fans decked out in red and black sweaters and sweatshirts. It also wasn't hard to see or hear that none of them were saying a word.

The chant got louder and louder. It was so loud that one of my teammates, Aaron McGee, thought I had brought my own cheering section to Memphis. Truth is I had no idea who those people were up there. Coach answered the call of the fans and put me in.

When I checked into the game the response was so intense I thought it was a home game. I played well enough, but it was nothing spectacular. When the game was over, I searched the stands again for a familiar face, and still couldn't spot anyone I knew.

Today I still wonder about that game. It makes me feel good to know that even outside of Cincinnati, someone had noticed my major strides.

CHAPTER 7

CAT WALK

I think that the best things about being a college athlete were the memorable life experiences I got when I was playing on the road. As a Bearcat, I saw and did many different things that I would never have done on my own.

The traveling was fun, but sometimes it wasn't so enjoyable after a big loss. Still, I cherished each and every experience, good or bad. Some of them were sad. Some were really entertaining.

One particularly entertaining event happened during my first season in the "Shootout" with our crosstown rival, Xavier University. I'd heard all the hype as a casual fan, but I never thought this one game could mean so much. The media and preparation were as intense as it gets. Radio, TV, and print reporters were everywhere, and the game was all they wanted to talk about.

As a Bearcat, if there's one team we never want to lose to it's Xavier. A loss to Xavier would always result in humiliation like you wouldn't believe. This particular year humiliation and humor would meet.

The year before, Xavier star guard, Lenny Brown, had beaten Cincinnati with a last-second shot. That game was on national TV, and the Bearcats were still No. 1 in the nation at the time.

We entered this game with revenge in our hearts. It was horrible to be called the second best team in Cincinnati. This year the game was being played on Xavier's home court, the Cincinnati Gardens. The atmosphere was electrifying.

As the game progressed, it quickly became evident that this would not be the year for revenge. Our star, Ruben Patterson, was ineligible, and Xavier took full advantage of his absence. We lost by twenty-one points.

After the game, the depressing locker room scene was weird. Livid with rage, Coach Huggins started in on Ruben, even though he hadn't played. He felt Ruben had not prepared the team in practice. Next he ripped into Fletch for having a bad attitude and not being a positive contributor to the team. Everything, absolutely everything, he had told us to do this game, we had not done. He was not about to let us forget it.

Like dominos we continued to fall. Next he nailed Bobby Brannen for his lackadaisical effort. Then came D'Juan Baker's turn. D'Juan had taken some ill-advised shots during the game, and Huggins criticized his leadership and shot selection.

Then came a moment I'll never forget. A still fiery Huggins turned to point guard John Carson, who was always at least 35 pounds overweight. Huggs hesitated, then said, "And Johnny, you're . . . you're just the hamburger king!" For a moment I couldn't believe what I had heard. I wanted to fall on the floor laughing, but I knew better.

As I tried to keep my composure, football walk-on Brad Jackson, a bom comedian, was shaking my leg hysterically. We both sat there trying to keep a straight face. The team doctors and managers behind Huggins were laughing.

I don't recall who it was that Huggins blasted next. All I can remember is sitting there, staring at the pudgy face of John Carson. He wasn't smiling, of course, and all I could visualize was him wearing a crown with a hamburger sticking out of his mouth.

When most people see Coach Huggins, they see a flamboyant, big bear of a man, in expensive suits, stalking the sidelines. For the most part, they're right, yet his on- court and off-court demeanor are completely different.

To me Huggins was more like a father figure, someone I admired and respected. Yes, he does have his moments. Sometimes I didn't agree with what he was saying, but I believe that disagreements are part of any father-son relationship. He got pretty intense on the side lines, but at half time he cranked everything up two notches.

My most memorable story about Coach Huggins came during the Iowa State game in the 98-99 Great Alaska Shootout.

It was half time, and we were not playing up to our potential. Huggins was conducting one of his normal half- time motivational speeches. He was sharing a few choice words with people, yelling, writing things on the board, the usual. Then it happened. Boom! Huggs snapped. The chalkboard became his enemy. He punched the board so hard that his hand almost went through it. He just kept yelling at us as if nothing had happened. As we were leaving the locker room, I saw Huggs lean over to one of the

team doctors and say, "I think it's broken."

It didn't take a Rhodes Scholar to know he was in excruciating pain. But he wasn't going to let us know he injured his hand. By the end of the game, his hand was swollen to the size of a melon. He had to have it wrapped and iced.

Alaska wasn't the first place where Huggs fought the chalkboard. The more I thought about it, Huggins squared off with the chalkboard on numerous occasions, and on many of those epic battles, I ended up caught in the middle.

I always had the best seat in the house. To me, sitting on the sideline was like being in your living room in front of a big screen TV with surround sound. The action was right there. And half time was like getting sent to your room for doing something bad, with your father following close behind. Trapped! No way to escape. No matter where you sat, you were just an arm's reach from your dad. Half time in the locker room with Huggins was a lot like that.

Sometimes he would get so mad that he couldn't even speak or put anything on the board. To release his raging inner tension, he would wind up and throw something at the board. Most of the time it was nothing more than a marker.

During these locker room explosions, I always sat in front of my assigned locker which happened to be closest to the board. I could tell when something was coming, and get myself prepared.

Whatever he threw would nearly always ricochet off the board and hit me in the leg, all to the amusement of the team and coaching staff who knew as well as I did that I'd get hit with something at half time.

One incident felt like a scene in a TV comedy. It was a conference game with Houston, and we were up big but not playing well at all. Half time came, and Huggins was 200% raw anger, an awesome sight to behold! He couldn't finish a sentence! Everything tumbled out in fragments . . . "You . .. what that.. . are you out of your ... I can't beli..."

Then there was a terrible silence. I had learned early that silence with Huggins meant something very bad might happen. He had a can of pop in his hand, and a little voice inside of me was saying, "Please put down the can. Put the pop can down. Come on, pick up the marker."

BOOMMMMMMMMMMMMMM!

The pop can left Coach Huggins' hand with great vengeance and furious anger, and struck the board with enough force to knock out Mike Tyson. My unfortunate seating arrangement left me covered in carbonated corn syrup. Once again I managed to perform my duties as a walk-on, and took one for the team. Because of where I was sitting, I managed to shield my teammate Kenyon Martin from the shower of caffeine-free diet cola.

But I never once complained about where I sat with the team at half time. I could have been one of the many UC students who put their life on hold for as many as two days to camp out for tickets. And everyone in line was not guaranteed they would get a ticket. So maybe my half time seat wasn't so bad after all.

To get back to the Great Alaska Shootout. We were in the final game of the tournament. The game was against Duke, the number one team in the country. I was sitting on the bench searching the crowd for a possible celebrity. This was nothing out of the ordinary, every now and then a famous face would turn up. While I had one eye on the game, my other eye got stuck on three of the most awesome visions I had ever seen.

They were in the front row, absolutely beautiful, model- like females, comparable to Pamela Lee Anderson, Halle Berry, and Jennifer Lopez. Each of these three goddesses wore a veil, and waved a sign saying, "Trajen, will you marry me?" If Trajen Langdon, Duke's phenomenal shooting guard, didn't want to consider the proposals, I'd definitely have no problem doing so, myself.

We won the game. When the celebrating ended and things had calmed down, I was surprised to learn that my teammates had also noticed the girls in the front row. One of the biggest games in UC's basketball history, and the whole team had been checking out those lovely divas.

We got our trophy, waved to the fans, and then the hunt began. Imagine fifteen jocks desperately searching the crowd for Trajen's groupies. We beat Duke, and now we were trying to take their women. Unfortunately, the girls were not to be found. But the Great Alaska Shoutout Trophy was just as beautiful in our arms!

Alaska certainly lived up to my expectations. I experienced things I will never forget. Nevertheless many of my most enjoyable memories came during bus rides.

We never took the bus on extremely long trips; for that I was thankful. So many characters were on the team that I don't think I would have survived a ten-hour road trip with them. Sometimes three hours on a bus with those wannabe comedians was long enough. Yet those characters made

every bus ride memorable.

We'd just beaten George Mason in the first round of the 98-99 NCAA tournament. Our team had lived up to expectations. We crushed George Mason! The bus was packed with coaches, wives, and children. The show we had put on the court was just a warm-up for the show to come.

Shawn Myrick, our point guard, started things off by making a beat with his mouth. To us, this wasn't anything unusual. We always rapped on the bus after a win. As a matter of fact, we did something a little out of the ordinary every time we got on the bus. But to anyone riding with us for the first time, this had to seem strange. It didn't take long for Melvin Levett to realize that Shawn's beat was his cue to break into one of his infamous bus-ride raps. However, this time things were a little different. Instead of sounding like a rap, the song turned into a military role call. Melvin shouted, "My name is Mel."

And we said, "What?"

"The helicopter."

"What?"

"I jump high."

"What."

"And you can't stop me."

Everyone busted out laughing. The verse was supposed to rhyme, but it didn't. Nor did it make any sense. The roll call continued, and everyone got a chance to say his piece. It was now my turn to recite an eloquent soliloquy.

I was one of the last to do the roll call, so I had time to think and I had a lot of material to work with. First, we had just received our per diem (daily allowance for food), and I had it in my hand. Second, I had just played in my first NCAA tournament game, and that was a really big deal.

The problem was that my big appearance in the blow out with George Mason was deflated when I shot two air balls. The guys teased about those shots all the way to the bus. With that in mind, I was ready for roll call.

I shouted, "My name is Al."

And they said, "What?"

"Yeah, and that's my name."

"What?"

"I shot two air-balls."

"What?"

"But I still got paid."

Then I waved my money in the air, and again everybody busted out laughing.

Speaking of money, the strangest bus trip occurred when we were playing a tournament in Las Vegas, the land of big money, big dreams, and big debt.

We were there for the Las Vegas Shoot-Out. We had just finished playing UNLV. After we showered and changed, we were supposed to meet the coaches and the rest of the staff at the Hard Rock Cafe.

Coming out of the hotel into the parking lot, I said, "Man, someone is bumpin'." I couldn't figure out where the sound was coming from. As we got closer to the bus, I said, "You got to be kidding me." When Kenyon Martin stepped in front of the bus, the door whooshed open and one of the songs of the famous rapper, Master P, came blaring out.

This was a rare bus. It was a rare bus equipped with a rare bus driver. He looked no older than one of us. That was so odd because our normal bus drivers were usually old guys who looked like their name should be Mr. Crabtree, similar to my grade school bus driver, who smelled like Ben Gay and would tell you to shut up for sneezing too loud.

When we got on the bus the driver politely turned the music down. Melvin Levett noticed the change in the volume, and impolitely said, "Hey, Man! You better turn that back up!" I knew then, that this was going to be a bus ride to remember.

The driver didn't just turn the music up, he turned the volume up to the standard listening level of a teenager, and that translates into, "too loud for anyone over the age of thirty-five." Then the bus began to look like a bad episode of Soul Train.

Can you picture a bus full of people whose average height is six-foot-six trying to make dancing look graceful? Besides that, there was no Gregory Hines on the team. I think that deep down inside it was every one of their dreams to become a rapper. As soon as they got their chance, they took turns rapping over the intercom system.

When we stopped at traffic lights, people started looking at us in total confusion. One lady driving along side the bus even took our picture. Either she was amused, or she thought that it was a bus hijacking story she could sell to Hard Copy.

When we finally got to the Hard Rock Cafe, the people in the parking lot had a dazed look of confusion. One of our team managers came up and said, "Why are you guys all sweating? Is the air conditioning broken on your bus?" Melvin looked at him and said, "No man, we just got off the Soul Train."

Bus trips, plane rides, and tournaments were some of the good times on the road, but the road also took me down a dark, uncertain path.

We played the University of Alabama/Birmingham during my first year in the 97-98 season. This was a transitional period for us since Ruben Patterson had just returned to the line up. Ruben was our star forward, but an NCAA violation kept him benched the first half of his senior season. Ruben was a little rusty, and with him back in the line up so were we.

Ruben still possessed a child-like giddiness that was clearly visible. He was like a kid in a candy store with ten dollars eating a hole in his pocket. He was my roommate on the road, and we usually talked till late in the night. But thisnight was very unusual.

Ruben had dreams of going to the NBA. He never talked about where he wanted to play, nor did he say what kind of car he was going to buy. The only thing that really seemed important to him was taking care of his mother.

I remember the glow he had while talking about his mother. He talked about all the great things she had done for him, and how she deserved to live a "glamorous life." She meant everything to him. The last thing he said before we went to sleep was that he wanted to buy her a nice big house. I soon realized how ironic that statement was.

I was out cold when I heard a knock at the door. It was five a.m., and I didn't want to get up. The only reason I did was the voice at the door said, "It's Coach Huggins." I stumbled across the room thinking "What did we do now?" Coach asked if Ruben was there and I said, "Yeah, he's back there asleep," wondering what NCAA rule Ruben had violated now?

Coach Huggins and Assistant Coach Rod Baker got Ruben up and took him into another room. I just lay there feeling the uneasiness. I heard Ruben crying as Coach Baker came out of the room, and told me that Ruben's mom had a massive heart attack and passed away last night.

I couldn't believe it. The news hit me real hard. Not even five hours had gone by since Ruben shared with me that he was going to buy his mom a house as soon as he got drafted into the NBA.

That morning, at breakfast, I had to tell everyone what had happened. I'll never forget it. Many players shared my disbelief. We couldn't believe that the only family Ruben had was gone. We all understood that this meant, for the time being at least, that we would have to become Ruben's family.

I saw a few tears escape from Coach Huggins's eyes. He was trying hard to keep his composure as he told Ruben he should go home on the next flight.

"No." That's all Ruben said, and everything was quiet. Coach Huggins said, "You need to go home." Ruben, in a calm tone of voice said, "No, my mom would have wanted me to play." And play is what he did! He played the best game of his college career. He had thirty-two points, seven rebounds, and three assists. Every time he would score he would point to the sky.

All of us on the team knew who he was pointing to, but none of the fans did. The fans were being typical, booing and saying cruel things, but that's to be expected at an away game.

I suddenly realized how much I admired Ruben, for his ability to block out all the distractions and overcome such a difficult situation. I remember the glow he had just the night before, but this time, tonight, the glow was his mother shining down on him.

I have never suffered a loss as great as Ruben's, but I had to learn, just as he did at life's crossroads, to keep focused on the path ahead.

Being a walk-on, lurking in the abyss of the subconscious, I would hear a voice that said, "Hey look at me, too,". It was not a voice that made me forget my role, but sometimes it cried out for a chance to be noticed.

After the black socks episode I mentioned earlier, I was always looking for ways to have fun. I figured the best way to accomplish this task was to change my appearance.

Dan Hoard, the Fox 19 play-by-play announcer, made mention of the full beard that I had been growing. He approached me after I had scored a career-high seven points in the Nicholls State game, and said, "I guess the beard must be lucky." I had never been one to believe in luck, but since he took such notice in my facial hair, I saw this as a perfect opportunity for reinvention.

It was the night before one of our home games that I decided to do a little trim work on my Grizzly Adams look. I'll explain this to the best of my ability in order to give the full effect.

First, I trimmed my beard real low. Then I decided it would be interesting to connect my side bums with my mustache. I didn't stop there. I decided to cut away the bottom of my goatee. The finished product, side-bums and all, looked like a big "W" on my face.

There was a film session that night. That was my first chance to try out my new look. I walked into the room, and everyone busted out laughing. Aaron McGhee said, "What's up, Butch?" "Man, you look like some biker dude named Butch that even I wouldn't mess with." Everybody laughed. Melvin added, "Wait until the fans see you tomorrow."

Sure enough the media had a field day with my new creation. When I checked into the game, Dan Hoard said, "How about the new look on Alex Meacham? He may not lead the team in scoring, but he leads the team in new looks." Anthony Buford, the other Fox sports announcer, said, "I think he kind of looks like the Artist Formerly Known as Prince."

Once again I had temporarily satisfied the voice from within that desperately cried out to be noticed. When I reflect on all of those memories, I finally see the big, overall picture. My paws have traveled down many different roads. Even if the roads would lead me over a cliff, I would always land on my feat with the grace of a cat.

CHAPTER 8

IN MY SHOES

Being a walk-on has changed a lot of things for me, especially the way that I watch other college basketball games on TV. I live for blowouts. Don't get me wrong, I like a good game, but a blowout gives me a chance to see others in my unique society of the walk-on athlete.

Most people turn off the TV during a blowout. Either they are satisfied that their team is going to win, or mad because their team just got crushed. That's the beauty of the whole thing. A blowout means that both teams are going to put in their walk-ons.

I was curious about what other walk-ons' experiences were like, and what stories they had to share. I found three in particular: Jerry Fitzgerald from DePaul University, Steve Masiello from the University of Kentucky, and Josh Pastner from the University of Arizona.

We were playing DePaul my first year as a walk-on, and we were up by thirty points. Melvin Levett gave me that get-ready-to-come-in look, so I knew that it was show time. It was my time to shine and it was my time to score. Since we were up so much, DePaul also put in their walk-ons, and that was the first time I met Jerry Fitzgerald. I knew who he was. As a matter of fact, I knew every walk-on in the conference from reading the media guides. This was the first time we played against each other, and his job was to guard me.

During a free throw we talked and he seemed like a real nice person. On our next trip down the floor he showed me how nice of a person he was, and hit a three-pointer right in my face. I knew I had to strike back. On our next trip down the court I told him, "I owe you one." The very next play I hit a three-pointer in his face. This was the beginning of our friendship.

I also became friends with DePaul's other walk-ons Brian Cashin and David Bruno, but because of our friendly rivalry, Jerry and I had a closer bond. From then on, it became a ritual that we would talk for a while during pre- game shoot around.

When DePaul came to the Shoemaker Center, Jerry, Dave, Brian, and I met at half-court for our usual discussion of life as a walk-on. Okay, so maybe we were asking each other who saw the girl in the front row. One of the managers came up and asked me if we were having some kind of "Walk-on Talk." After he said that to me, I looked forward to playing DePaul and having more "Walk-on Talks."

No. 20, Jerry Fitzgerald, is a five-foot-eleven guard out of Oak Park, Illinois. He was a high school star, and had dreams of playing basketball for the DePaul Blue Demons. I wanted his insight for this book. He was a walk-on for four years under two coaches.

For a walk-on, a change of coaches can be a difficult situation. You learn a new system, you try to figure out a new coaching style, and you wonder all the time if you're

still going to have a spot on the roster.

Jerry's first two years as the lone walk-on were under Coach Joey Myers. During this time his emotions were up and down. He said, "I didn't feel very close to the team. It was unfair. There were obvious differences in the treatment between the scholarship players and me." One incident in particular almost drove him to quit.

Every walk-on looks at their schedule and circles the games they're sure to get in. DePaul was playing one of those games against Eastern Illinois during Fitzgerald's sophomore year. Jerry said, "This was one of the games I had circled." He did what any good walk-on would do, and invited all of his friends and family.

DePaul went up by twenty points toward the end of the game, and the crowd started chanting his name. On the bench you get this feeling that people are looking at you, but when the crowd starts chanting your name, you know it. That's when you know they are waiting to see you check in.

As time began ticking off the clock, Jerry sat patiently, and wondered when he would get in the game. With each passing second, the chant faded and so did Jerry's hopes. The final seconds ticked of the clock. He was upset as the coach told him, "Sorry we couldn't get you in."

Personally, I have been there before. It hurts. It hurts because you can't let people know that you're hurt. You are supposed to be happy that your team just marked another victory in the record books, but deep down inside at that moment, you just don't care. Jerry wanted to leave the team.

The following season DePaul hired a new coach, and Jerry changed his mind about leaving. With the addition of

Coach Pat Kennedy from Florida State, walk-ons Brian Cashin and David Bruno made Jerry want to stay on the team. He ended up having a good relationship with Coach Kennedy, and Brian and David became his best friends.

I often wondered how it felt to play on a team that struggled for so long. Jerry said, "It is frustrating because you want to win more than the guys ahead of you." Even though I played for Cincinnati, a team that won over twenty games a season, I often felt the same way.

Aside from all the bad things that happened, Jerry remembered a lot of good times. He recalled his senior night game experience against Duke. It was the largest crowd ever to see a college basketball game in the state of Illinois. He entered the game to a standing ovation and scored two points. But, his best memory was when they beat Cincinnati (No. 3 in the nation at the time) at the Rosemont Horizon. Whenever we met, he was sure to remind me of that game.

I asked Jerry, after four years of playing division one basketball, what was his definition of a walk-on. He said, "A guy who knows his role, and will do anything to make the team better."

Jerry is a team player, and he proved it during his four- year career. After two years of fierce rivalry, I gained a deep respect for him, and I'm certain that he will continue to be a team player in whatever he does.

Having Bearcat blood running through my veins automatically eliminates me from the list of die-hard Kentucky fans. However, I must admit that I have watched quite a few of their games and even on occasion found myself cheering for them. I would always watch to see if

No. 4, Steve Masiello, would get into the game.

Steve is a six-foot-two guard out of White Plains, New York, who after the 99-00 season was a walk-on for four years at the University of Kentucky. The unique perspective that Steve brings to this book is that he knows what it's like to win a national championship.

At the age of 13, Steve received an extraordinary invitation from the New York Knicks point guard, Mark Jackson. It said, "Hey kid, why don't you come and watch one of our practices sometime." Steve accepted the invitation and enjoyed it so much that the one time invitation became a regular event.

The New York Knicks' head coach at the time happened to be the same guy that every die-hard Kentucky fan will undoubtedly say is the greatest coach ever, Rick Pitino. Pitino made the kid from White Plains a ball boy, and an immediate friendship was formed between the two.

Pitino followed Steve's progress through high school, all the way up to his senior year when he averaged 8 assists and 34.5 points per game. It looked as if Masiello would attend Davidson College on a full scholarship. But at the last minute, Davidson's tough academic requirement didn't allow him to attend.

Coach Pitino heard what had happened, and gave Steve a call to ask if he wanted to come to the University of Kentucky as a walk-on. Steve described it like this: "Your life-long girlfriend breaks up with you, and then Cindy Crawford asks you to go out on the same day." This was a done deal for Steve, and he hoped that his walk-on status wouldn't be permanent, and that he would eventually receive a scholarship.

When Steve spoke about Pitino, he talked about him with the same respect that someone talks about his father. A walk on's journey is never an easy one, but in talking with Steve it seemed like Coach Pitino had made it easier.

When Coach Pitino called a team meeting to tell his players that he would be leaving for the NBA, Steve said, "It was a very emotional meeting, and the guys were pretty upset." "We were happy for him going to the NBA, but sad for us because we were losing such a great coach." Losing a coach is an altogether different experience for a walk-on. Steve was worried about the transition, because walk-ons are never guaranteed a spot.

The change of coaches didn't affect Steve. He ended up having great success with the new coach, Tubby Smith. Coach Smith immediately recognized Steve's contributions, and awarded him the "Reggie Hanson Sacrifice Award."

When UK went to play Canisus in Buffalo, New York, Mayor Masiello (no relation) declared it "Steve Masiello Day." Steve's efforts had not gone unnoticed. For his hard work and dedication in practice, he was rewarded. A few games later, against Wright State, Steve was put in the starting line-up.

One time I asked him, "What are your goals when you don't get much playing time?" He immediately said, "Win a national championship!." "What's it like to win a national championship," I questioned. He struggled to put it in words, then said simply, "The feeling is so great you want to have it again and again."

"As an individual player, what are your goals?" I continued. Steve said, "I'm the only senior on the team, so my job is to be an effective team leader." But, "How can

you be a leader if you're a walk-on?"

Steve was quick to tell me he wasn't fond of being called a walk-on, because of the negative aspects that come with it. "People think that walk-ons can't play just because they don't get the same TV time as the scholarship players. That's frustrating because I know 1 can play." He went on to say that he didn't let it upset him because he knew his role and accepted it.

During the summer of 1999 Steve Masiello was granted a scholarship for the 99-00 season. Coach Tubby Smith had this to say about Steve, "What a joy he is to have on this team. His leadership is very important and needed on this team. I have as much respect for Steve as anyone because it's not easy to come to practice every day knowing his minutes will be few. But he has a chance to contribute."

You can bet that Steve Masiello is making a strong contribution to whatever "team" he is on now.

During the 98-99 basketball season we went out to gamblers' heaven to see what lady luck had in store for us and played in the Las Vegas Shoot Out. We were scheduled to play UNLV. Arizona was also there rolling the dice against Iowa State. Even though we played second I didn't have time to gamble, but I did have time to sit and watch some of the Arizona game. The whole time I was watching, there was a player on the bench who stood the entire game. The player was Josh Pastner, a five-foot-eleven guard from Kingwood, Texas, who was known as 'the kid who never sits down." I had heard about Josh from one of our former players, Brian Bland, who knew him from Texas. We were at study table one night, and Bland showed me an article in USA Today on the "Wanna Be Coach," Josh Pastner.

I was warming up for the UNLV game, and I looked up in the stands and saw that Josh was sitting down. I was amazed. Not that he was sitting down, but that he was talking to the Chicago Bulls general manager, Jerry Krause, and the new Bulls head coach, Tim Floyd. There was a lot of laughing and smiling going on so I figured that they were pretty good friends.

I knew right away I should talk to Josh about his experience as a walk-on. I found him to be one of the most mature, well rounded college students I had ever talked with. He described the beginning of his college basketball career as "The toughest two weeks of my life! Not the physical things, but earning the respect of the teammates." I knew what he was talking about!

Josh, like all of us, often thought about quitting, but that would go against his big plan. His big plan was, and still is, to land a head coaching job somewhere. He knew that playing for a high profile team like Arizona would help him do that. He also said that Arizona stand-outs, Michael Dickerson, Mike Bibby, and Miles Simon helped make his situation smoother.

Josh told me a story of how a late night shoot around turned into one of the best opportunities of his life. He went to the gym late one night, and Mike Bibby was also there. Mike was there because he had a dream of playing in the NBA, and he knew that in order to achieve this goal he would need to spend more than just the normal practice time in the gym. Josh, a student of the game, made a deal with Bibby.

The deal was if Mike practiced shooting with Josh for two hours a day, his (Mike's) dream would come true. The deal went on for two years. No matter what was going on, no matter what time it was, they dedicated two hours a day in the gym. Bibby used his time with Josh to work on his game, and Josh used his time with Bibby to work on his coaching. Mike Bibby is now in the NBA, and gives Josh credit for making him a better player.

One thing that I found quite fascinating about Josh was during the pre-season of 96-97, Josh told Coach Lute Olson, "We will win the championship this year." He said that he just had this feeling, and so he began telling the other players everyday, "We are going to win the championship." Josh's bold statement came true that year.

Is Josh Pastner a psychic? No, but he has a dream. His dream is to win a national college championship, as well as an NBA championship, as a head coach. Josh has finished his undergraduate studies, and his masters. He is now working on his Ph. D. School is definitely important to him. Josh proved his quest for academic excellence by winning Arizona's Academic Award and the Most Inspirational Award during his junior year.

Josh was offered a scholarship, but turned it down so Arizona would have an extra spot for transfer player Loren Woods, from Wake Forest. With the huge sacrifice that Josh made, he gained the respect of the whole program. I asked him what his definition of a walk-on was. Josh broke it down as, "An extraordinary person who has the desire to do extraordinary things, and does them."

Josh prepares himself every day to be a coach, and he feels that his walk-on experience has taught him, "The importance of hard work, taking nothing for granted, and learning to sacrifice for the little things." With his father, Josh coaches a Houston AAU select team called the Houston Hoops.

He wants to coach so bad, that he applied for the head coaching job with the Los Angeles Clippers. He knew that the Clippers' attendance was down, and they were a young team looking for a spark. Josh figured he was that spark. What better way to get fans back in the stands than to have a young team coached by the youngest coach, ever, in the NBA.

Josh didn't get the job. There is no doubt, however, that before too long he will achieve his dream. He is one of those guys that, if you know him, it just becomes a question of ""when" he's going to make it happen.

After interviewing these three, I have come up with the perfect definition of a walk-on: "Jerry, Steve, Josh, and Alex."

CHAPTER 9

MENTAL MARATHON

The game of basketball is 90% mental, 10% physical. Many people don't understand this. When you examine today's basketball players, you will often find equal physical talent, but a separate mental approach. How often do we see someone who looks physically dominant, but fails to compete with the other players of equal size and ability?

Why does one succeed, while the other fails? For the most part, success comes down to a positive mental approach to the game.

As a walk-on, there was one asset crucial to my success. It was not how high I jumped, or how fast I could run. For me, as well as many others, success boiled down to one word—Confidence! I had to believe that I could compete! That I was worthy of a chance, despite the fact that I had never played one full year of high school basketball. My confidence would have to separate me from many others who, although talented, made an unsuccessful bid at becoming a walk-on. Not just at the University of Cincinnati, but at hundreds of Division I schools across the country.

As a Bearcat, I saw it happen several times. A player would lose confidence in himself, and get benched. If he regained his confidence, his playing time would increase. If not, it would be a battle with me for a prime seat on the bench. This was a sad reality, but a reality non-the-less.

At the Division I level the mental stress is so intense that, at some point in the season, tempers will flare up and arguments will arise. Not simply with the opposing team, but within your own team. It was shocking, at first, but I soon came to understand that with the Cats, it was just another day on the job.

It happened right away my first season! I expected players to lose their tempers, but it was different to see the coach and a player go at it!

It was a home game. Half-time seemed to come fast at this particular game. We weren't playing well, so we all expected Coach Huggins to give us one of his famous half- time rip-jobs. For some reason, I suspected that Melvin Levett would be the center of Huggs' attention, and sure enough, he was. Big time!

Coach started in right away on Melvin. He exploded in a tirade of insults. Melvin was selfish! He was supposed to be a team leader, but he wasn't! Maybe they ought to rename the team "The Levetts!" I thought that last remark was kind of humorous, but what happened next was really bizarre.

As Huggins continued, he touched a sore spot. "Melvin, you just don't care," he said, in a way only Huggins could say it. As if someone had questioned his manhood, Melvin jumped out of his chair and challenged Huggins. The helicopter had gone into a tailspin.

As they got into a shouting match, Ruben stepped in and grabbed Melvin, while assistant coach Baker pulled Huggins away. Still upset, Melvin was dragged out of the locker room to cool off.

As I sat there taking this all in, I said to myself, "What the hell is going on here? Is this normal?" After a brief moment, Huggins regained his composure and proceeded to "tell off' the rest of the team as if the incident had never happened.

As we walked back on to the court for the second half, I found it strange that no one seemed upset about anything. True enough, no blows were thrown, but if words were punches, this would have been a double knockout. As a first year player, I was a little naive about this kind of Bearcat camaraderie. Just before the buzzer, 1 calmly asked Fletch, "What was that all about?" Fletch gave me that "you rookie" look and replied, "Same old !*#@, just another day!"

A year later, the "same old !*#@" came back. This time the roles were different. Fletch was Huggins' target, and I was the seasoned veteran. The newcomer was Alvin Mitchell, who sat there, a carbon copy of me the year before. After the dust settled between Fletch and Huggs, Alvin asked, "What was that all about?" I gave him that "you rookie" look, and replied, "Same old !*#@," just another day!"

What I learned from these occasional outbursts was that at the Division I level, the season is long and the stakes are high. At some point there is going to be an explosion. It's nothing personal, but good or bad, it gets your attention. After all, even close families have internal squabbles. But when all is said and done, you're still a family. The Bearcat team was no exception.

These verbal sparring matches also gave me a better understanding of coach Huggins. He is a tough, no- nonsense man, and he realizes that his confrontational style can sometimes be overbearing, especially on a young athlete who believes he is trying his best.

Knowing that everyone has limitations, Coach allows his players a certain leverage to speak their own mind. Even if it sometimes seems out of line. I admire Huggs for this, and without it he wouldn't be Huggs and get the respect he gets. But maybe he should consider a new nickname: Huggs?

Coming back to my feelings on confidence. In the NBA you have a collection of the best 350 basketball players in the world.

So, why do only a few reach the level of Oscar Robertson, Michael Jordan, or Larry Bird? Are they really more talented, or just more confident. I'm convinced it's confidence that separates the good players from the really great ones.

Likewise with coaches. Certain coaches just know they can put a winning team together. Since Coach Huggins came to Cincinnati, he's won 20 or more games each season! This is a phenomenal record, but not surprising. Huggins' mental approach is specific and singular. He came to show the guys how to win. He knows he can win.

He restored prominence to a once failing program, and earned such respect that the Bearcats are now televised nearly every game.

Although TV time is a flattering compliment to a program's success, it can also be disruptive. Most often the distractions take place when a player is looking for self- gratification through a 3-second video clip. Coach Huggins is well aware of how destructive a camera can be. I remember how he would warn us about these personal agendas. If he ever caught you playing to the camera, he would have a few choice words for you, and you were not likely to ever do it again!

For all its problems, television can often be valuable in learning the game. Whenever I talk to younger players, I try to emphasize the importance of studying the game. Not just the highlights on ESPN or FOX, but the strategy that made the highlight possible. TV now makes the big picture very clear, and gives today's players real opportunity for mental preparation.

Although I never became the high school player I wanted to be, I studied the great players often, searching for that mental edge. I wanted to know what made a great player great. Most often I found that great players are also great students of the game. They often watch endless hours of film, not just of their opponents, but of themselves as well.

They critique their game constantly, searching for any improvement. If their jump shot is off, they study their technique and make the necessary adjustments. If they're having a problem with their footwork, they search the tape for an answer to the problem. The one important factor about reviewing film is this: It never lies!

The camera's eye is brutal, and it's a constant reminder that things can always get better.

One thing that gets lost in today's game is self-criticism. Every basketball player thinks he's the next Michael Jordan.

The shoes, the swagger, and even Jordan's tongue wagging have been copied at every level of basketball. But what everyone seems to have missed about Jordan is how critical he has always been of himself. This is probably the one attribute that lifted him head and shoulders above the other NBA stars.

Jordan was always searching for ways to improve his and the team's performance. He was never comfortable with being simply "one of the best": he wanted to be "the best!" He wanted to stand alone. And through hard work, dedication, relentless self-study, and constant goal-setting he achieved that position.

I remember watching him over and over with the Chicago Bulls. His physical gifts were obvious, but it was his mental approach that intrigued me most. I was obsessed with the way he seemed to enter every game as if it would be his last.

Even in the latter stages of his career, when there was nothing left to prove, he was always challenging himself. He never gave an inch, even when his skills were apparently diminishing. The constant remark about Jordan from other players throughout the NBA was, "He wants it more." He wanted to win, and was willing to sacrifice personal glory for victories. In the end, his personal goals were met, with six NBA championships and a legend that may never be equaled.

Success in basketball starts in the mind and is transferred to the body. You have to mentally dominate if you want to physically dominate. If you rely on physical skills alone, you will always find someone just as talented as you.

Being a walk-on gave me a unique view of the game. Of course I would have preferred to play more, but I am comfortable with the thought that everything happens for a reason. On the bench I had the opportunity to make many important observations about the game and its players.

I watched how Bobby Brannen, a player not so athletically blessed, could evolve into one of the best players in the country during his senior year. Bobby was a poster boy for what dedication and mental toughness can do. He never said much, but his work ethic spoke volumes.

Each day he battled against Danny Fortson and Art Long, both more physically talented than he, but neither had the confident mental approach that Bobby had. And despite being knocked down time and again, he got back up as strong as ever. Eventually he became one of the most respected players ever to wear a Bearcat uniform.

I'm no basketball guru, but I feel I do understand how the game is supposed to be played, even if my personal contribution to the Bearcats' success was limited. Great players sometimes make lousy coaches. Average players sometimes make great coaches. With that in mind, I'm confident my career options will remain open.

CHAPTER 10

WALKING AWAY

Everything happened so fast, I rarely had an opportunity to reflect upon it all. Practice, games, school assignments. Before I could grasp the meaning of the moment, it was all but over. It was time to walk away.

Senior night had arrived with the speed of NBA star Allen Iverson on a fast break. Two years had gone by and there I was facing my final home game as a member of the UC Bearcats. Over the past two seasons, I had developed a fondness for Shoemaker Center, much like someone would for a place they called home. I suddenly realized that my home-court advantage was slowly slipping away.

With my last night at "The Shoe" rapidly approaching, I decided that I would try to implement the same game plan that had comforted me throughout both seasons. Despite the significance of this game, I would not stray away from my routine or pre-game rituals. Sunflower seeds and apple juice were a must. My drive to the Shoe, including streets, turns, and landmarks, a given.

Call it superstition, call it game-day strategy, but whatever it was that had sustained me, I was certain it would have to be a part of this special evening. It's strange how you never truly appreciate something until you're faced with losing it. I was now coming to grips with the reality of my journey. At some point, it had to end.

As my roommate, Sam Dunn, and I, left for the final game, we had little to say to each other. Usually we talked a lot. I think he too was aware of just how important this night was to me. Along our drive to the Shoe, Sam was sure to make the same turns and past the same restaurants that we had identified on previous game nights. Even as we arrived at the back of the arena, the same security guard was there to give me a hard time about getting in. For reasons unknown, it seemed he never figured out that I was a member of the team, and not some crazed lunatic searching for an open door. While his forgetfulness often irritated both Sam and me, this night seemed special. On this night he would just become one of the many memories that I would take away from my experience as a walk-on.

Walking through Shoemaker Center that night, I came to the realization of just how important time is. Time is the only element that waits for no one. It has no respect for stature, race, lifeline, looks, even potential. I suppose in basketball terminology, 'time" has never been known to call a "time-out." And although I knew this moment had to take place, I was desperately waiting for a break in the action.

It was a weird feeling to pass those familiar ushers and staff for the last time. As I walked by Mrs. Lemecke, who was always seated at the entrance, I remember her saying, "We're going to miss you, Alex". I paused for a second, and replied, "Don't worry, I'll be back."

Ten steps later was her husband, an usher who always asked me about tonight's game strategy and who was the opposing player to watch. He looked me straight in the eye and said, "I sure enjoyed watching you play for the past two years." Somehow, on this last night of my career, every moment became a one-time affair.

The game itself was probably the least item of importance. We were playing our Conference USA rival, Louisville, and I was confident that we'd win. For me, shaking hands, receiving hugs and well wishes was my #1 priority. If there was one thing that did concern me, however, it was the possibility of finishing my home career on the bench.

My parents and grandmother were in attendance, and I wanted them to feel what I'd felt for the last two seasons. I wanted them to hear the noise and the chants of "Al-ex, Al- ex," as I approached the scoring table to check in. I wanted them to see the students who were dressed up in home-made "Alex" T-shirts and painted sideburns like mine.

My parents deserved more than just a walk-on the court. They deserved to share my experience as a Cincinnati Bearcat. After all, if it were not for them, I would never have made it to this moment.

They set the groundwork for me to excel and were my prominent role models. Even though my mother was apprehensive about my plans to be a walk-on, they have always been there and never discouraged me from pursuing my dream.

As this final night unfolded, I realized how my much I had inherited from my dad and mother. My dad is the picture of organization, always on time, and well-liked by everyone. My mother is the hardest working individual I've ever known. For her, working a task through to its completion is automatic.

With the game in full swing, I looked out over the crowd, wondering if I'd wake up from it all. Was this some type of cruel dream? Another Twilight Zone moment? Had all this really happened, or was I simply a victim of unrealistic aspirations?

As I continued on my mental journey with my mind still set on dream-status, I turned left and looked down the bench pondering what lessons I could take away from my experience Lessons not simply applied to basketball, but more appropriately, lessons for life.

What could I take away from a powerful figure like Coach Huggins? The screaming? The unforgettable stare? The moments when I thought his head could spin around? Determination! That's what I would take from Huggins!

Everybody thinks Coach Huggins is some out-of-control dictator. After two years' experience, I arrived at a slightly different opinion. To me "Huggs" is simply a man who will not accept being out-worked by anyone. He may lose a game, but it's never because of a lack of preparation. Although his yelling and on-court theatrics can be distracting, if you look beyond the choice phrases, you'll often find an answer that makes sense. I guess the best way to describe Coach Huggins is "Straight-no-Chaser." And like the drink, he can be an acquired taste.

I turned away from Coach Huggins, and to my right was my off-court coach, Jerome, sitting in the front row. It was only fitting that he was there for my last home game.

If it hadn't been for Jerome, I would never ever have made

it to this night.

A few days earlier I'd offered him a gift to show my appreciation for his help. He explained to me that the best gift I could give him was to pass along the knowledge he gave to me. Somebody told him. He told me. And now it was my job to tell someone else. As he put it, "Pass on the 'hand-me-down' knowledge to the next man."

With the game approaching its final minutes, I began to wonder if I'd play at all. It was my last chance to influence anyone with the same dream I'd had. Maybe somewhere in the crowd of 13,176 people, there was someone searching for that edge.

Time was now running out. The game was close and I was convinced that Coach Huggins had forgotten about me. As chants of my name echoed throughout the Shoemaker Center Huggins finally turned to me and gave me the sign. Thank God, I thought, he remembered. There was only about three seconds left on the clock, but I was determined to make the most of it.

I entered the game to a standing ovation. I wanted to score! I got the ball in my hands, and put up a shot. It didn't go in and then the horn sounded. That was it. My home career as a Bearcat was now history.

As I walked off the court shaking hands and waving to the crowd, I knew it was important to savor the moment. Before the game I had a talk with my roommate, Sam, about jumping into the stands like some NFL players do after a touchdown, but he said, "That's not you."

After a seemingly endless post-game chat from Coach Huggins, I came out to meet the crowd. Even the students who had made signs and T-shirts about me were there for some final good-byes. They gave me all the items they'd made up over the past two years, and for me, nothing could have been more special.

While the temperature outside was frigid cold, a few friends and I decided to walk back to my apartment, ignoring Mother Nature's wrath. I chose the pathway I typically walked, that is, before the cold forced me to ask Sam for a ride. We took the same streets, passed the same landmarks, even walked at the same pace. Only this time I knew it was over. After tonight, there would be no more long walks home. Tonight I had made my final stroll past the ushers on my way to the locker room. The cheers, the band, and the fans would soon become a silent memory. In a strange way, I'd even miss Coach Huggins post-game tirades.

I will miss all the good and bad times of my two-year experience. The longest trek in my life, ever, was over. But somehow, deep in the back of my mind, I knew this was only the beginning.

Being a walk-on for two years taught me that the walk never ceases. The pace may change, the scenery may be altered, but step-by-step, the journey remains. Life as a Cincinnati Bearcat was preparation for the walk ahead. At some point everyone has to step into their journey.

One day I'd like to be able to tell my children how I endured. Not simply as a walk-on for the basketball team, but how I endured life's walk-on, where second chances come at a high price and mistakes are just part of the process.After all, I made it through a journey no one thought possible. Step-by-step, I survived a "Walk of a Lifetime.

Made in the USA
Middletown, DE
23 August 2024